LAW, FREEDOM, AND STORY
The Role of Narrative in Therapy, Society, and Faith

John C. Hoffman

Rarely has an author illuminated in one book an aspect of religious study with attention to so many disciplines. John Hoffman skillfully interrelates the fields of psychology, mythology, anthropology, literature, and New Testament studies to show their common use of narration techniques. Hoffman explains how the storytelling nature of myths, parables, and psychotherapy seeks to heal and to bring wholeness to both the individual and to a social grouping.

Bringing into this discussion the tension between law, the stabilizing factor of a society, and freedom, the spontaneous and creative urges that move outside of social order, Hoffman shows how rituals function to affirm the order of the culture in which they exist, yet, as they open up the realm of the imagination, they provide the possibility for disruption. For as long as fantasy is a part of narration (both in telling and hearing) the social order can be both criticized and superseded.

Hoffman clearly sets his work within the genre of Crossan, Perls, Jaffe, Turner, Grimes, Buechner, and Eliade. Carefully examining the work of Tom Driver and John Cobb, he expresses the need to go beyond traditional structures and formulations in order to move theology closer to narrative. A narrative form, Hoffman argues, can both affirm faith and invite believers to transcend its expression and break free of its strictures, providing for an ever more dynamic theology.

John C. Hoffman is Professor and Head of the Department of Religious Studies at the University of Windsor. He is also the author of Ethical Confrontation in Counseling.

LAW, FREEDOM, AND STORY
The Role of Narrative in Therapy, Society, and Faith

LAW, FREEDOM, AND STORY

The role of narrative in therapy, society, and faith

John C. Hoffman

Wilfrid Laurier University Press

This book has been published with the help of a grant from the Canadian Federation for the Humanities, using funds provided by the Social Sciences and Humanities Research Council of Canada.

BT
78
.H55
1986

Canadian Cataloguing in Publication Data

Hoffman, John C. (John Charles), 1931-
   Law, freedom, and story
     The Role of Narrative in Therapy,
   Society, and Faith

Includes biographical references and index.
ISBN 0-88920-185-4

1. Storytelling – Religious aspects – Christianity.
2. Religion and literature.   3. Law (Theology).
I. Title.

PN49.H64 1986   230.01   C85-090867-1

Copyright © 1986

WILFRID LAURIER UNIVERSITY PRESS
Waterloo, Ontario, Canada   N2L 3C5

86 87 88 89 4 3 2 1

Cover design by David Antscherl

Printed in Canada

No part of this book may be stored in a retrieval system, translated or reproduced in any form, by print, photoprint, microfilm, microfiche, or any other means, without written permission from the publisher.

To
    Jeanetta, John, and Sandra,
    important chapters in my story

Contents

1 Why This Book? 1

2 The Parables of Jesus: A Study of Storytelling 15
    Crossan on the Parables 16
    A Philosophical/Theological Critique 25
    A Literary/Phenomenological Critique 31

3 Story and Fantasy in Psychotherapy 39
    The Narrative Character of Self-Understanding 40
    The Telling of Stories 46
    The Reappraisal of Fantasy 54
    Fantasy and Therapy 60

4 Structure and Anti-Structure in Social Processes . 71
    Structure in Social Process 72
    Turner's Concept of Liminality 78
    Liminality and Social Change 81
    Nomization and Liminality as Threat 89
    Creative Liminality in the Social Process 92
    Positive Liminality 96

x / Law, Freedom, and Story

5 The Dual Transcending of Law 103
    Law, Gospel, and the Transmoral (Works vs Grace) 105
    Law, Gospel, and the Transnomic (Structure and
        Anti-Structure) 109

6 Towards a Transnomic Theology 125
    Driver's Parabolic Theology 127
    Cobb's Renomic Theology 138
    Story and Transnomic Theology 151

Index 161

1
Why This Book?

There is an old story of a tourist travelling in the south of Ireland who stopped a farmer on the road asking directions to Dublin. "It is Dublin you would be visiting," said the farmer, scratching his head. "Well now if I were wanting to go to Dublin I wouldn't have started from here." If the truth be known, the present work did not start from here. In a written form it started with chapter two and only after long months did it venture into chapter three. As an exercise of the mind, however, it began long before any of this.

For some years now there has been a growing interest on the part of scholars in the role of story as a medium for the transmission and articulation of religion. Story, both verbally recounted and acted out in ceremonies and rituals, has come to be recognized as a virtually universal and potent vehicle for faith. A wide range of scholars from many disciplines have turned their attention to this phenomenon. They have developed various dimensions of the total reality from the point of view of psychology, history, comparative mythology, sociology, literature, and so forth. The present work, then, is offered as another contribution to this ongoing discussion.

We have long been aware that religions have told stories but now a new focus has been given to the centrality of this type of experience within faith. One can discern a twofold interest here. Part of it relates to the actual experience associated with the telling of stories in religion and its relation to storytelling in general. Here one enters into an exploration of the narrative character of religious experience and awareness. The other part of the interest details the actual telling of stories in a faith context, the kinds of tales told, the occasions upon which they are recounted, the various modes of their expression, including their acting out in individual and social ceremonies and their visual representation in art. Simply to cite a few examples, one finds such works as Frederick Buechner's *Telling the Truth*, John Dominic Crossan's *The Dark Interval: Toward a Theology of Story*, Mircea Eliade's *Myth and Reality* and many others, Sam Keen's *To a Dancing God*, Wesley Kort's *Narrative Elements and Religious Meaning*, William Lynch's *Christ and Apollo: The Dimensions of Literary Imagination*, James McClendon's *Biography as Theology*, Michael Novak's *Ascent of the Mountain, Flight of the Dove*, Peter Slater's *The Dynamics of Religion*, Sallie McFague's *Speaking in Parables*, James Wiggins's *Religion as Story*.

In *The Religious Experience of Mankind*, Ninian Smart identifies six basic dimensions, as he calls them, of humanity's religiousness: the ritual, mythological, doctrinal, ethical, social, and experiential. As employed by Smart, the mythological dimension becomes essentially the narrative element of faith. He reminds us that "in origin, the term 'myth' means 'story.'"[1] In his analysis, central to the life of religion are both story and ritual enactment. Some debate exists among scholars as to whether myth or ritual is primary or whether one does not inevitably imply the other. Smart asserts, for example: "The meaning of ritual cannot be understood without reference to the environment of belief in which it is performed."[2] Indeed one can argue that ritual is basically enacted story, dramatic presentations of elements of the mythos. Yet it seems clear that the acting out of faith occurred long before any written record of narrative existed. Whether one says that religion was danced or narrated first, there seems to be a consensus that mythos and ritual preceded theology and formal systems of doctrine. Religion has existed without any significant doctrinal development but not without this twofold narrative expression. Humanity told and dramatized faith before it was ever systematized. This in no way denies the importance and power of the doctrinal dimension through religious history but it does suggest a certain priority for the dramatic which I suspect is both temporal and ontological.

---

[1] Ninian Smart, *The Religious Experience of Mankind* (New York: Charles Scribner's Sons, 1969), p. 8.
[2] Ibid., p. 7.

One can divide Smart's mythological dimension into a number of narrative styles. Myth can be limited—as it is by many scholars—to world-defining stories which purport to take place outside our space and time, involving the gods or the primal ancestors or the last being. The most popular conception here would be the Greek myths or the many variants of creation stories. The opening chapters of Genesis function as such for Judaism and Christianity. The native peoples of North America recount a rich diversity of such tales, differing in tone from Genesis in that they convey a far more intimate relationship between the human race and nature. In many cases, dogs, coyotes, bears, or birds are the immediate creators of our species. The Chinese stories of the god P'an Ku reflect a commonly found theme of sacrifice wherein the god dies to bring about creation. In this account humanity is humbled by the assertion that we were made from the lice which fell from P'an Ku's hair. To be sure, not all myths deal with creation. Others detail the healing, the transformation, the redemption of humanity or the world, describing cosmic battles between the gods and the forces of evil or chaos. The early interpretations of the Cross with the figure of *Christus Victor* frequently were set forth in such mythological form.

The field of religious narrative also includes legends, stories told as if occurring within our world and history but making reference to some extraordinary, supernatural intervention. The lives of the saints, so popular in the Middle Ages, are full of such narratives. The Chasidic tales of Judaism contain many examples of legends, as do narratives in Buddhist and Sufi tradition.

Some stories told in religion could be called natural fiction, stories of this world without any supernatural incursions nor claiming to reflect actual events in history but which witness to a truth, evoke a moral or spiritual response, provide guidance to the sojourner. The parables of Jesus, Pilgrim's Progress, or the biblical Ruth are typical examples. Were one to listen to the story of the Prodigal Son and then ask if the far country was north or south, the storyteller would despairingly shrug his shoulders, realizing that the narrative import had been lost. Many of the Sufi narratives are also natural fiction.

Finally, religious traditions, especially in the so-called historical religions—Judaism, Christianity, and Islam—tell stories that are taken to be detailed accounts of actual events and that become central to their faith understanding. The Gospels, while including mythological, legendary, and fictional elements, are basically presented as faith histories of the life of Jesus. Large portions of the

4 / Law, Freedom, and Story

Hebrew scriptures are essentially historical, as is the account of the life of Mohammed and his reception of the Koran. To be sure, even in the so-called philosophical religions of the East there are historical tales, such as the enlightenment journey of the Buddha. Obviously, in a rich variety of forms, stories have been and continue to be a medium of faith.

A study of ritual life in religious traditions reveals that many of the more important ceremonies are, in fact, quite dramatic presentations of the major stories of the faith. To be sure, some more limited forms of activity present them only indirectly and partially. The Catholic lighting a candle before the figure of Our Lady of Guadalupe would tell little to the uninformed, yet even here the act finds its meaning in terms of a rich framework which is deeply infused with narrative. But again, central to many religions are key rituals and ceremonies where the definitive stories of the faith are dramatized. The Muslim pilgrimage to Mecca involves re-enacting portions of the saga of Abraham, Ishmael, and Hagar, as well as events in the life of the Prophet. The Buddhist ritual for the ordination of a monk sees the novice set out first in fine clothes and hailed as a regal figure, only then does he change to the saffron robes of the monk and go forth with his begging bowl. All of this clearly retells the story of Prince Gautama's venturing forth from the splendour of his father's palace, discovering the reality of suffering and death, and turning from ease to the ascetic life of a monk. The Hebrew Seder relives the original Passover meal, in this case a re-enactment which includes a verbal retelling of the story as each portion of the drama is presented. Of course, the Christian Eucharist recounts in words and actions the events of the Last Supper and their place within the whole Passion narrative.

It is interesting to think, at this point, of many of the so-called quasi-religions, those social institutions and ideologies that operate to set the basic framework of understanding, values, and lifestyles for many of our contemporaries. I refer to the secular faiths, Nazism and Communism being powerful examples in the twentieth century. These in their own way exhibit strong ritual and mythological dimensions. Maoism, to take one concrete example, has, in the story of the Long March, a narrative which plays a role closely paralleling that of the Exodus in Hebrew faith. Indeed, just as the Exodus became a symbol as well as an event, so too Chinese leaders can speak of new calls for discipline and action to build the classless society as a summons to begin a new Long March. The stories of the heroes of the Revolution stand as inspirational examples for the Maoist peasant, as did the lives of the saints for the peasants of medieval Europe. One even finds elements in the Chinese versions which bear a distinctly supernatural flavour. The powers of evil, represented by the old, corrupt social order which the Revolution overthrew, are presented dramatically in the famous ballet of the white-haired girl and graphically in the massive *Rent Collection Courtyard* sculpture which depicts the cruel landlord's oppression of the masses. The Long March itself became the focus of a ten-act play, offering a faith interpretation of the event on the fortieth anniversary of its completion.

All this is offered merely as a reminder for religious scholars, or as a cursory introduction for those who are not, of the vast range and power of story in humanity's religious experience. There can be no doubt that religion has drawn upon the storyteller to convey the faith.

This, of course, is the kind of information that the detached observer of religion can become aware of and academics can discuss. The origin of the present study, however, lies in more than a knowledge of this fascinating collection of stories. More accurately, it springs out of that other dimension of the study of narrative and religion, namely, reflection upon storytelling experience with a view to discovering what this may say about religion, given its strong allegiance to this medium. Do stories function simply because they are a memory aid or an enchanting vehicle? Is it perhaps that human experience has a narrative quality itself? Does the power lie, as Wesley Kort suggests, in the fact that the narrative elements of atmosphere, character, plot, and tone are particularly suited to express religious insights? In short, why does story work and what does this say about religion?

My own conviction that story does work, my experience with the power of story, became the catalyst that triggered this study of narrative form and religion. Some years ago I attended a colloquium of scholars from many disciplines dealing with storytelling and religion. For the first day and a half or perhaps longer—it seemed very long at the time—we listened to careful analyses of the nature of myth, the possible influence of various story types, and several psychological theories of narrative. All this was very enlightening and scholarly, yet it seemed like a denial of the very reality it claimed was important. I remember asking myself whether any of these people had ever heard a good story or a joke, even a bad joke. Finally, sometime during the second day (it may have been sooner; memory remembers selectively, but it was after a long spell of intellectualism), a young woman came to the podium to give the next address. She instructed us about how this collection of scholars was to respond with cheers and boos on command at the beginning of her tales. She even carried a tambourine! Having awakened us, she began to recount stories from the traditions of North American native peoples. Gone was the sense that I desperately needed a coffee to stay awake! I was caught up in the world, fantasies, symbols, and movement of the Inuit of the Canadian Arctic or the Navaho of the southwestern United States. Something of their life, truths, and values became real for me at that moment. The experience was repeated later in the conference when a Jewish raconteur, steeped in the tales of the Chasidim, again brought us into that world of enchantment.

Since that time I have increasingly endeavoured in my own teaching of various courses to awaken in students a deeper sense of what we were exploring through the medium of storytelling. Classes of students who look apathetic at best literally come alive when I put on Indian beads to recount the story of Coyote and the Clearwater Monster or when I take a story from the Bible which they have often heard and present it in the style of the Bedouin sage. In a similar way, in the more casual setting of retreat centres and while working with adults with a wide range of age and education, I have told stories offering a narrative approach to faith. In all this I have found a virtually universal response to the power of story. One literally sees people change under the spell of the storyteller—although I am far from expert at this—and the change often lasts long after the tale has ended. Such is my experience with the power of narrative for the teaching of religion and, as one who stands in a religious tradition, with its power for the confession of faith and the evoking of faith in others. Narrative, I am convinced, is both powerful in and central to creative humanness, which is also the goal of religion. Thus this work represents, in the first instance, another attempt to explore the phenomenology of storytelling, to seek the grounds of its power, and to reflect on the theological significance of it all. Many works have been written but I am convinced that there is yet more to the magic of narrative dynamics which could have import for the whole task of theology and faith. Such is the point at which I really began this "trip to Dublin."

I would, however, acknowledge another source of this study, one which was not focal to my attention at the outset. I had just published my first book, one in which I had sought to deal with the place of ethical confrontation, the moral challenge, in a counseling context. The work grew out of a deep conviction that when counselors, in order to foster acceptance or "unconditional positive regard," seek strenuously to avoid all moral judgments, inevitably they become both ethically and therapeutically inadequate. I remarked in that work:

> Therapy, after all, is conducted in a real world where human beings do not just lie on the analyst's couch, express their feelings openly in the safety of the therapy group, or receive electrical shock treatments. It is part of a world in which people dream and build, curse and kill, laugh and love, suffer and die. To be mentally whole is to be able to cope with such a world. If you and I would be mentally whole, we cannot deny entire dimensions of reality and live as if there were no question of moral values.[3]

I sought to articulate the nature of the dynamics of moral functioning, and proposed the possibility of a non-moralistic morality and thus of ethical confrontation in counseling which would not destroy its therapeutic power. I rejected the assumption that one cannot heal and rebuke at the same time, arguing that it is possible to confront, even vigorously, bearing witness to the counselor's ethical understanding while maintaining a healing relationship.

The work was well received. One or two critics, however, saw in it a covert expression of tyranny. It was deemed by them finally to be still moralistic and my counseling punitively ethical. I wondered, like many authors, if these reviewers had read the right book since I had thought to argue strenuously against such things. But fortunately I had a good collection of positive reviews. A critical review, published more recently but which I read before beginning this work, was written by a colleague with whom I do not always agree but whose thought I must always respect. He argued that the problem of the work lay in its beginning with the concept of law, a concept that suggests "that humans possess a knowledge of good and evil, which is embedded in that which is considered to be lawful, rational, or normal in a given culture." He argued that I operated on the assumption that "human consciousness is basically correct in the knowledge of good and evil when it follows the laws embedded in nature and clarified by scriptural revelation." Again I felt that my first effort had not been understood. Had I not stressed that a counselor can only bear witness to his perception of moral truth and not claim to possess some absolute grasp which could be imposed on all others? In some critical responses I suspected that there was an image of Luther in the

3 John C. Hoffman, *Ethical Confrontation in Counseling* (Chicago: University of Chicago Press, 1979), p. 3.

reviewers' thinking such that the word "law" innately carried a negative connotation which it did not convey to me. In the later criticism, the charge was other than moralism. The fault was seen to be not in a moralistic employment of law but simply in the use of law at all. Law, even when not moralistic, was considered to be inevitably legalistic. There was, in a sense, a double reality of law to be encountered; law raised more than the problem of moralism. Thus there was a residue from this earlier study, standing as an issue which I felt that someday I must address, but this was not where my own interests lay at that moment.

My own professional involvement at the university meant that the time available for counseling was necessarily reduced while the focus upon teaching was greatly expanded. I was personally captivated by the power of narrative in relation to religion both as a clue to the phenomenon of faith and as a medium of instruction. As this study progressed, my attention turned to certain aspects of narrative dynamics which became for me a major and exciting element in the hearing and telling of stories, and a source of their power and creativity for religious expression and understanding. To my surprise, this insight also proved to be the key that allowed me to carry further my earlier discussion of law in the life of faith. This new perspective did not alter the position developed in the earlier study but allowed me to expand it, to develop a more precise or richly articulated perception of the role of law in relation to gospel and freedom, one which would more clearly refute the charge that law of necessity means legalism.

In the Sufi tradition we find the figure of the Mulla Nasrudin, the whimsical, wise fool about whom many tales are told. Much of the tradition is reminiscent of the Chasidic materials of Judaism. Indeed there are examples of the same story finding a place in each. Let me recount one short incident from the Sufi collection.

A man saw Nasrudin searching for something on the ground. "What have you lost, Mulla?" he asked.

"My key," said the Mulla.

So the man went down on his knees too, and they both looked for it. After a time, the other man asked, "Where exactly did you drop it?"

"In my house."

"Then why are you looking here?"

"There is more light here than inside my own house."[4]

4   Idries Shah, *The Exploits of the Incomparable Mulla Nasrudin* (New York: E. P. Dutton, 1972), pp. 26-27.

One could argue that like the Mulla Nasrudin I chose to look where the light was brighter. (At least the light of interest and excitement was more intense.) But in looking there, in studying the dynamics of narrative experience, I have discovered in fact a key that I believe helps to unlock the dynamics of moral functioning in counseling, even to cast considerable light upon the dynamics of human functioning in general. Thus the second element in the prehistory of this book, though not a matter consciously directing the study at its inception, has become a significant element in its final form. The narrative dynamics I want to articulate relate immediately to the role of law, in its broadest sense, for human life, including ethical confrontation in counseling. We shall discover a need to distinguish a twofold function for law in human experience and the power of narrative to nurture those functions most creatively. I shall have cause to argue in the latter parts of this work that these very dynamics raise matters of crucial importance for the style and form of theological argument. Traditional expressions of theology are themselves in danger of being open to the broader charge of legalism, which was raised by one of my own critics.

Let me sketch the form of argument in this book. In keeping with its thesis concerning the importance of the narrative dimension in the articulation of theology, I want to present my own position logically but also in a way that reflects the developmental process in my own thinking. I shall, therefore, present material in an historical order. The one exception is that a large portion of the final chapter which discusses the Christologies of Tom Driver and John Cobb was actually written in first draft prior to the arguments developed in the previous chapter. Yet even here the order has historical accuracy for I found it necessary first to clarify the issues examined in the previous chapter before I could properly interpret the significance of the Cobb and Driver analyses, which set them within the total theological context that was finally evolved.

I begin with some current New Testament scholarship concerning the parables of Jesus, particularly with the work of John Dominic Crossan. The parables are, of course, an obvious example of the use of narrative in religious tradition. The New Testament debate was whether these stories were told for the purpose of creating an image of God or the religious life, a concrete content, or whether, as Crossan claims, they offered no content, being told basically to disrupt all such ideas, to shatter all understandings. I came to believe as a result of this discussion that one of the important and powerful aspects of narrative dynamics was actually the ability to create a structure within which to live while at the same time inviting one to experience the freedom to transcend, to disrupt, to challenge that order. Adopting Crossan's terminology, I have labeled this the mythoparabolic character of narrative experience.

In keeping with the methodology employed in the earlier work, I turned to examine what support could be found for this thesis through exploring the use of story-like experience in psychotherapy. This, however, is not a purely random choice merely because there is a personal light of interest here. Religion, like psychotherapy, seeks to be a change agent, to heal, to bring wholeness. Thus in searching for the power of stories in therapy, their capacity to be a vehicle of change in that context, we might hope to find some insight into their transforming power in a religious milieu. It was naturally a matter of considerable interest to find what I interpreted to be evidence for both the use of story to convey specific content and its introduction as a means of disrupting the interpretive framework, the world, of patients. Here was the same dual function of narrative found in the debate over the intention of Jesus in telling parables. Moreover, with the use of fantasy, therapeutic impact was found for story in moments that appear to transcend this polarity of affirmation and disruption. It has been argued by some that therapy does not really begin to occur until the therapist and patient can "play" together. We have here a suggestion that a fuller experience, perhaps even a fuller humanness, lies beyond the polarity of affirmation and disruption. One also finds an echo of this in Crossan's work when he speaks of the experience of transcendence which is made possible through the parabolic. The fully positive character of this *transnomic* moment, as I shall call it, did not become clear to me, however, until I encountered its more explicit articulation in sociological studies. Nor is it apparent to me that therapists very often use story with this whole range of narrative functions in mind. While I have argued that it is the nature of story to be mythoparabolic, I find that most therapists use such techniques either as an alternative mode of providing insight, i.e., as mythic, or as a medium to disrupt accepted position, i.e., as parabolic. They do not consciously seem to be using them, for the most part, with both functions in mind.

In the course of these earlier studies which followed much of the style of my previous work, I came across references to the writings of Victor Turner and particularly to his concept of "liminality." He describes this as that moment in human experience that allows people to stand outside the boundaries of their society's world-taken-for-granted with all its accepted meanings. In Crossan's terms, it has a parabolic character. Turner develops this material in his analysis of ritual, especially in the more primitive societies. Subsequently, he expands his understanding of liminality, seeing in it a basic element in the social process generally. His work was naturally of interest to me. This concept of liminality raised again the idea of the creative role of the disruptive in human life, in this case seen in relation to communal development rather than individual therapy. His focus upon ritual brought me once more to the question of story when I remembered that rituals can be seen as enactments of stories or story fragments. Thus in the fourth chapter I turn my attention to the function of rituals and ceremonies in the social process, where I found the same narrative dynamics. Stories can operate in society to affirm, strengthen, or define social structures, roles, and shared meanings. They may also disrupt, challenge, and even overthrow them. In some cases one, in some the other, is the primary intended function of these social dramas. This difference is illustrated by contrasting the society-reinforcing ceremonies of Santa Fe as described by Ronald Grimes, and the disruptive impact of the liminal rituals and the institution of pilgrimage, as outlined by Turner. Turner further enriches our discussion by clarifying the dialectical character of this relationship between affirmation and disruption or, in his terms, between structure and anti-structure, which is central to narrative experience. The ordering and the disordering, the mythic and the parabolic, as described by Turner, are both essential elements in human functioning. The power of story, one can now argue, lies partly in its capacity to mediate both of these vital dimensions of our experience.

Moreover, Turner outlines for us the positive value of the parabolic, the disruptive or disordering moment. He sees its creative function in the service of order and structure, yet he claims for this moment a positive value *in se* which moves beyond the negative connotations of disorder and disruption. The transnomic, in my terms, is more than a disruption of structure; it offers also the potential for a higher form of human relationship which Turner calls communitas. Here we find a fuller experience of community, one that transcends the limitations of social structures, roles, and definitions to reach a more immediate encounter. In retrospect, one can see intimations of this, as already indicated, in Crossan's hope for transcendence through the medium of the parabolic and the suggestion that therapy truly begins when we enter the realm of play.

These studies of narrative dynamics have made it necessary for me to acknowledge a more complex relationship between law and gospel, law and freedom, than was developed in my earlier study. In the fifth chapter this insight is developed in terms which distinguish a dual relationship between gospel and law. It begins by recognizing the relationship between gospel and law in its *moral* function, law as an imperative. It is, of course, law in this mode which raises the spectre of moralism and leads us in the earlier work to affirm Tillich's call for a transmoral conscience, a conscience which grants one the right to be prior to or apart from moral achievement without denying the validity of the moral imperative. I now feel the need to acknowledge the relationship between gospel and law in its *nomic* function, law in its ordering, structuring, interpretive function, law which sets the inevitable and necessary context within which one lives. I argue that we need to find not only our right to be beyond the justified claims of the moral law but also a freedom in relation to law as *nomos*, as the framework within which we live and conceptualize reality. This is required both to develop a critical distance, permitting the reappraisal of our world-taken-for-granted, and to open us to that fuller experience of communitas, play, transcendence. These categories are then applied briefly to expand upon the discussion of the place of law in counseling. The nomic function of the law in this context becomes the essential nature of law in the life of faith.

The final chapter deals with the implications of this thesis for the presentation of theology. What form of theological expression most adequately witnesses to the traditions of faith while also evoking the liberty of the children of God? What style of doctrinal articulation can serve not only as guidance but equally as a call to freedom in relation to those very assertions? I examine at some length the attempts by Tom Driver and John Cobb to explore this question in relation to Christology. How can Christians be faithful to Christ and yet be free? How do they relate to the traditional understandings of Jesus of Nazareth, thus being in some meaningful sense recognizably Christian while avoiding bondage to that tradition? How does one conceptualize a Christology which invites one to transcend it? In their terms, how can we avoid bondage to a Christ of the past in order to be able to respond to a Christ of the present-future? I find much to agree with in both Cobb and Driver. Each represents an advance in the development of a transnomic theology. Nonetheless, neither gives a fully adequate mode of theological expression. I argue that it is a question not only of content but also of style. Theology must move closer to a narrative form which can simultaneously affirm a faith and invite the believer to transcend its expression, to break free from bondage to detail. The embryonically historical/narrative character of the presentation of my own argument is at best a weak beginning in the development of such a theological style. Still it is offered out of a deep conviction of the need for theology to find a mode of expression which recognizes the imperative to express the faith in a way which calls beyond the form of its expression.

One final word. The materials presented in this study come from quite disparate fields: New Testament criticism, psychotherapy, sociology, and theology. In each case, my discussion is restricted largely to those issues that bear directly on the mythoparabolic character of narrative experience. Nevertheless, I have invariably tried to present the material in a manner consistent with the style and interests of the various disciplines. Thus I hope, for example, in my treatment of fantasy and therapy, that counselors will discover fine points of interest for their practice which go beyond the specific focus of the present endeavour. Similarly, in critically examining Crossan's analysis of Jesus' parables, I offer my interpretation of the epistemological assumptions operative in his thought.

But enough of prologue. Let the "story" begin.

2
The Parables of Jesus: A Study of Storytelling

As I have suggested, stories, both spoken and enacted, have always been a significant medium for the preservation and transmission of faith. Many attributes of narrative experience have probably been involved in this long history. Many dimensions of the impact of tales upon both the teller and listener have contributed to the power of story in our lives and thus to its choice for this religious function. The ability of story to entertain, to invoke the child in us, to catch our fantasy, all play a role. It is, however, the special attributes of story in relation to the structuring of our understanding that I highlight in this discussion, a quality that I found most intriguingly developed in some current New Testament studies on the parables of Jesus. This chapter will take the form of an examination of New Testament research, but only to the depth necessary for our basic concern with the nature of narrative experience. Hence, we shall not delve, for example, into the intricacies of textual criticism.

The issue was first raised for me in an interesting little book, *The Dark Interval* by John Dominic Crossan. There Crossan offers a picture of narrative not as a means of structuring or ordering reality to provide a framework within which to think but as a means of disrupting the order of reality, challenging all structures and meanings. Specifically he introduces this in relation to the teaching and life of

Jesus, claiming that the basic impact of both Christ and his words was disruption rather than affirmation. From a New Testament point of view, then, Crossan's work offers an important perspective on the teachings of Jesus, but from the point of view of our study it also makes us ask significant questions concerning the nature of narrative experience.

Rather than presenting a new image of God and human destiny, Crossan suggests that the teachings of Jesus oppose all images, questioning not only the established religious world view but any and all religious visions. The Incarnate Word is one of disruption. In Crossan's terms, Jesus is not a new myth but an explosive parable, not a new content for faith but a challenge to all content, preparing the way for an encounter with the Transcendent and thus for true faith.

This is an important corrective, I feel, in the interpretation of the Gospels. However, I want to use Crossan to bring to light issues of importance for theology and the study of religion. In particular, I would like to explore the nature of narrative experience, the hearing and telling of stories via Crossan, that we may see how peculiarly suitable it is as a medium for religious expression, especially its potential both to affirm and to disrupt our world view.

Crossan on the Parables

Crossan's understanding of the parables quickly emerges in his treatment of the Good Samaritan, possibly his favourite example. Traditionally it has been interpreted as setting forth a model of human goodness, the neighbour who responds in love to the needs of another. As Amos Wilder puts it concerning the Good Samaritan and the Rich Fool, these parables "are straight narratives about a given individual case, ending with an application." In short, they are "example-stories."[1] Similarly, Dan Via remarks, "The behavior and attitude sketched in The Good Samaritan and The Rich Fool (example stories) are not comparable to or analogous to what man should do or avoid but are exactly what he should do or avoid."[2] Thus the parable has been understood to paint a picture of goodness. Such is the natural, automatic interpretation, Crossan allows, when we read the story in its Lucan context, opening with the lawyer's query about inheriting eternal life and ending with the admonition

1 Amos N. Wilder, *Early Christian Rhetoric* (Cambridge, Mass.: Harvard University Press, 1971), p. 72.
2 Dan Otto Via, Jr., *The Parables* (Philadelphia: Fortress Press, 1967), p. 12.

"Go and do likewise." These standard readings date back at least to Luke himself.

In contrast to this tradition, Crossan offers the thesis "that the present context of the Good Samaritan parable . . . is not original and therefore cannot be used to interpret the meaning of the parable for Jesus."[3] Read apart from this context, the story takes on a radically different sense. It becomes a tale meant to startle the hearer. The Samaritan clearly remains the central figure, but the modern reader misses the point because the terms "Levite," "priest," and "Samaritan" no longer hold the emotional connotation that they did for first-century Jews to whom the Levites and priests were leaders of the religious establishment, the Samaritan a socioreligious outcast. To grasp its message we need to update the cast of characters. We might, for instance, tell a Northern Ireland republican about a nun and a member of the IRA who passed by while a member of the UDA stopped to render assistance. The primary impact of the parable, then, is not to affirm that we should help people in need but to disrupt our assumptions concerning who are the good and the bad. According to Crossan:

> the internal structure of the story and the historical setting of Jesus' time agree that the literal point of the story challenges the hearer to put together two impossible and contradictory words for the same person: "Samaritan" (10:33) and "neighbor" (10:36). The whole thrust of the story demands that one say what cannot be said, what is a contradiction in terms: Good + Samaritan. . . . When good (clerics) and bad (Samaritan) become, respectively, bad and good, a world is being challenged and we are faced with polar reversal.[4]

Assuredly, the Samaritan did a good thing, an action to be imitated. He is an example for us.[5] But if that were the primary point of the narrative, it would have come with greater force for Jesus' listeners had the roles been reversed: ". . . if the story really intended to encourage help to one's neighbor in distress or even to one's enemy in need, would it not have been much better *to have a wounded Samaritan in that ditch* and have a Jew stop to aid him?"[6]

3 John Dominic Crossan, *In Parables* (New York: Harper & Row, 1973), p. 58.
4 Ibid., p. 64.
5 Crossan points out that the Old Testament contains examples of actions even more exemplary. 2 Chronicles 28, for instance, tells of an episode in which kindness was shown to a beaten attacker. It is as if the man on the road to Jericho drove off his assailants and then tended to the wounds of one not able to flee.
6 John Dominic Crossan, *The Dark Interval* (Niles, Ill.: Argus Communications, 1975), pp. 105-06 (his emphasis).

Such is the essence of parable for Crossan. It entails a reversal of normal expectations, an overturning of a world-taken-for-granted, a disrupting challenge to cherished assumptions. In this light he seeks to interpret all parables and increasingly the teachings of Jesus generally. But let us pursue this further by looking at other examples, by comparing Crossan's treatment with that of Dan Via who represents the older, traditional approaches.

Via and Crossan agree that Jesus told parables in order to communicate and not, as assumed in Mark 4:10ff., to conceal the truth *"in order that* certain men might not be able to understand, repent and be forgiven."[7] They differ, however, as to the message to be communicated. Crossan sees the purging disruption of our religious understanding, while Via finds content in the message, an interpretation of the human situation. In the parables, Via sees the portrayal of two contrasting possibilities for human life: destruction and fulfillment. Drawing upon classical literary categories, he distinguishes tragic and comic parables. Though Via, like Crossan, begins with a study of the parables, he too subsequently extends the analysis, applying it to the whole New Testament which he believes interprets life as comedy (in Paul) or tragicomedy (in Mark).[8] In Crossan's terms—to which we shall return—Jesus becomes not the new parable but the new myth. How do the parables look with these contrasting assumptions?

The parable of the Workers in the Vineyard tells of labourers hired at various times of the day who all receive the same wage that was originally promised for a full day's work. Via finds in the narrative both tragic and comic elements. From the standpoint of plot it is a tragedy that depicts the lost opportunity for full life for the disgruntled workers hired early in the morning. In the end they are banished by the householder. "Because of their impenetrable legalistic understanding of existence, grounded in the effort to effect their own security, they excluded themselves from the source of grace."[9] From the thematic standpoint, however, it is a comedy that affirms that God grants us the right-to-be as a free gift, an act of generosity, not dependent upon human merit. From this perspective the parable becomes an allegory pointing to the graciousness of God. The story thus holds in tension the tragic and comic possibilities of human life.

7 Via, *The Parables*, p. 8 (his emphasis).
8 Dan Otto Via, Jr., *Kerygma and Comedy in the New Testament* (Philadelphia: Fortress Press, 1975), passim.
9 Via, *The Parables*, p. 154.

"[W]hile the ultimate meaning of life is God's gracious dealing, man may yet bring about the tragic loss of his existence."[10]

To be sure, Via acknowledges the challenging note in the parable, the assault on much traditional piety. "Our very existence depends on whether we will accept God's gracious dealings, his dealings which shatter our calculations about how things ought to be ordered in the world."[11] By contrast, it is this disruption of our assumptions rather than the proclamation of an existential decision for or against God that is the ultimate import of the parable for Crossan. It is a "reversal parable." The story "is not about goodness but about surprise," not about the grace of God but about the folly of our religious understanding.[12] Hence, he concludes, Via does not recognize the full, disruptive power of the parable. "God also shatters our understanding of graciousness and that is the most difficult of all to accept. What comes across most forcibly... is that this parable shatters utterly the normalcy of [life]."[13] It is not content but the assault on content that Crossan finds.

For most casual students of the New Testament at least, along with the story of the Good Samaritan, the other most widely known parable is that of the Prodigal Son. Here again we find the same contrasting interpretations in Via and Crossan. For Via the parable conveys information. It tells us something of the relationship between God and ourselves. Assuredly, one must not be simplistic about this. Via rejects allegorical interpretations wherein the Prodigal stands for publicans and sinners, and the elder brother for the Pharisees. Yet for him it still speaks of the prevenient love of God which makes repentance possible. Once more Via recognizes the note of surprise, the transcending of all expectations, the challenge to our natural assumptions concerning God, human nature, and goodness. Like the Prodigal, we are "incapable of knowing what possibilities for good might come to [us] until they do come."[14] To this extent the story is disruptive. Yet it remains fundamentally an affirmation, the presentation of a view of life. The tale of one man's journey from being lost and dead to being found and alive reflects an option for all. So Via calls this parable, "Jesus' classic comic story [in which] death is assimilated and overcome, and the note of joy is finally sounded."[15]

10 Ibid., p. 155.
11 Ibid., p. 154.
12 John Dominic Crossan, *Raid on the Articulate* (New York: Harper & Row, 1976), p. 161.
13 Crossan, *In Parables*, pp. 114-15.
14 Via, *The Parables*, p. 169.
15 Ibid., p. 146.

Against this, Crossan once more emphasizes paradox and disruption. He argues that we should not accept the Lucan context, with its reference to tax collectors and sinners, and the parables of the Lost Sheep and Lost Coin. The Prodigal Son parable must be allowed to make its own point. When read in this way, Crossan believes that it is clearly another reversal parable which ends with the Prodigal as the honoured guest at the banquet while his dutiful older brother stays outside pouting. "It was not originally, as Luke now makes it, an example of how to act in the face of divine mercy but a parable inviting our imagination to a polar reversal of expectation."[16] It was originally not a portrait of God but a questioning of all making of divine portraits.

Obviously not all parables of Jesus immediately lend themselves to interpretation as reversal stories. Crossan's first work, *In Parables*, actually distinguishes two other general groups, parables of advent and parables of action. His basic emphasis on Jesus' disruptive intent, however, comes to dominate his treatment of these stories as well. I shall examine only his treatment of the latter category.

Eight stories of Jesus are presented under the heading, "parables of action," which are subdivided into two groups of four. The first group tells of good and successful servants being rewarded while evil, slothful ones are punished. Perhaps the best known example in this cluster is the story of the Talents, which Via sees as a classic tragic parable: "In the fear of the one-talent man we see the anxiety of one who will not step into the unknown. He will not risk trying to fulfill his own possibilities. . . . He started as a free man, but he refused to be responsible."[17] By themselves such stories are obviously not disruptive; they lack the paradox central to Crossan's thesis. He does find polar reversal, however, when they are related to the second group of parables of action where wicked and slothful servants are rewarded.

The account of the Wicked Tenants who murder the heir in the hopes of gaining the vineyard is a case in point. While allowing for some allegorical references to Israel's disobedience, Via takes the parable to be essentially a story which finds its meaning internally as an expression of the tragic possibilities for human life: "When the Wicked Tenants is seen as a parable of unfaith, then sin becomes man's self-centered effort to reject any and all limitations which the being and will of God impose upon him."[18] Crossan totally rejects

16 Crossan, *Raid on the Articulate*, p. 111.
17 Via, *The Parables*, pp. 118-19.
18 Ibid., p. 137.

any allegorical interpretations. Moreover, he does not consider Jesus' question about what the owner will do and the subsequent account of the villains' punishment as a part of the original narrative. (To do so, he believes, would be an attempt to set the story right.) He chooses, instead, the version found in the Gospel of Thomas where immediately following an account of the murder is the admonition to listen well. The parable then becomes "a deliberately shocking story of successful murder."[19] It is a tale of "lethal if prudential efficiency, of murderous violence which precluded quite obviously any usage of such stories as moral examples."[20] We have now, indeed, a dramatic reversal of expectations and religious assumptions, even as we find in the story of the Unjust Steward. Evil triumphs. Yet this is a reversal so massive as to amount virtually to an alternative religious vision. For Crossan the real meaning and the reversal occur when we set in juxtaposition the two groups of action parables.

> The parables of action all challenge one to life and action in response to the Kingdom's advent.... In the eight parables of the Servant cluster a theme is presented in ordered normalcy and then is just as carefully reversed and shattered. Like a wise and prudent servant calculating what he must do in the critical reckoning to which his master summons him, one must be ready and willing to respond in life and action to the eschatological advent of God. But unfortunately, the eschatological advent of God will always be precisely that for which wise and prudent readiness is impossible because it shatters also our wisdom and our prudence.[21]

Polar reversal is maintained. In this case, however, we must assume that those hearing the parable of the Talents would think of it in relation to the other stories which are its polar opposite. The parable by itself would not convey its proper message.

Clearly Crossan's treatment of the parables assumes the activity of an editor suitably modifying the initial form of these stories. And, in fact, he attempts to demonstrate the occurrence of such a transforming process by which the essentially disruptive character of the tales has been softened. When the central character of a story is obviously doing something which is morally good, it is easy and natural, he suggests, to turn the parable into an example story, a spiritual paradigm. The Good Samaritan is a classic instance of this. If, on the other hand, the story, at the literal level, recounts morally neutral

19 Crossan, *In Parables*, p. 96.
20 Crossan, *Raid on the Articulate*, p. 163.
21 Crossan, *In Parables*, pp. 119-20.

events or even natural phenomena, it does not lend itself immediately to such interpretation. One would hardly read the parable of the Sower as an account of the proper agricultural techniques for Palestine. But the Markan record of that parable illustrates precisely what can be done. The story becomes an allegory, referring usually to the actions and purposes of God. Crossan's claim is that in some instances we can see this process at work in the existing texts, a case in point being the parable of the Great Feast where we find that both styles of textual modification have been used.

Crossan believes the original story was quite simple and that each of our present versions represents interpretive additions. It tells of a spontaneous dinner party; the meal preparations are underway even as the host begins to invite his friends. With such short notice, all have legitimate reasons why they cannot attend. So the host, likely angry primarily with himself, sends for whomever can be found to share the banquet. Although at one time strongly contrasting parable and allegory, Crossan now speaks of allegorical parables and interprets this story as such. The story speaks of the Messianic banquet and the Kingdom of God. Nevertheless, its message is essentially one of disruption; it is another reversal parable.

> Can you imagine, asks Jesus, a situation in which all the invited guests are absent from a banquet and all the uninvited ones are present? This is fundamentally amoral and invites the hearers to recognize a situation of total reversal: the invited are absent, the uninvited are present. As parable it provokes their response to the Kingdom's arrival as radical and absolute reversal of their closed human situation.[22]
>
> Or, as Jesus might have said, the Kingdom of God will strike you as being as nonsensical as a dinner with all one's friends absent and only strangers present.[23]

Each of the existing versions has modified this story to give it more than this disruptive or startling character. Luke and Thomas moralize it. Luke offers the positive note with an insertion of the reference to the blind and lame. Crossan sees this as a clear attempt to tie it to the Lucan context. Just before recounting this parable, he records Jesus' admonition not to invite friends and kinsfolk to dinner, those who can repay the hospitality, but to invite "the poor, the maimed, the lame, the blind, and you will be blessed" (14:13-14). The story becomes an appeal to care for the needy, to exercise true

22 Ibid., p. 73
23 Crossan, *The Dark Interval*, p. 119.

Christian case law clearly becomes problematic, but a new possibility presents itself.

> Jesus' set of three situations represents case parody, a deliberate comic subversion of the wise and prudent necessity of case law.... Jesus is not offering case law, however ideal or radical, but he is challenging his legal tradition, like the book of Ruth before him, in the form of case parody.... [In these and similar passages we must avoid all] framing commentary which mutes their comic challenge and attempts to turn them into that which they originally subverted, back, that is, into case law itself.[24]

In a similar manner, Crossan sees Jesus as offering a "comic subversion of wisdom"[25] though his interpreters, both evangelists and some modern translators, have tried to "solve" these paradoxes. By comparing various versions, Crossan decides that the original saying of Jesus was probably "For to him who has will be given, and from him who has not will be taken away."[26] The tidy mind rebels! If one has nothing, what can be taken away? So Q puts the proverb right by adding to it: "from him who has not, *even what he has* will be taken away" (Luke 19:26). Similarly, Crossan believes Jesus said: "Whoever gains his life loses it, and whoever loses his life gains it." Tradition was unhappy with this "dark aphorism." So some versions were modified and spoke of those losing their life "for my sake" (Matt. 10:39) or "for my sake and the gospel's" (Mark 8:35). Once again the paradox that loss is gain and gain is loss has been emasculated. As they first stood, however, these proverbs were an end to proverbial wisdom. "Jesus is using paradoxical aphorism or antiproverb to point us beyond proverb and beyond wisdom by reminding us that making it all cohere is simply one of our more intriguing human endeavors and that God is often invoked to buttress the invented coherence."[27]

It is not Crossan's intention to argue that the evangelists and others were deliberately producing a distortion of the gospel message. They were able to turn the parables of Jesus into example stories and allegories because the paradox had taken a new and dramatic form for them in the person of Christ. "The parabler [had become] parable. Jesus announced the kingdom of God in parables, but the primitive church announced Jesus as the Christ, the Parable

24 Crossan, *Raid on the Articulate*, pp. 67-68.
25 Ibid., p. 69.
26 Ibid., p. 71.
27 Ibid., p. 73.

charity. With his closing insertion about tradesmen and merchants not entering the places of the Father, Thomas highlights a negative moral concerning the failure of the rich and preoccupied to heed the call of God. In contrast, Matthew takes the route of allegory. He too sees it as referring to the Kingdom of God, but he also considers it more than simply a reversal parable. It is a dramatic presentation of *Heilsgeschichte*. The murder of the servants and the subsequent destruction of the killers and their city, inserted by Matthew, alludes to the rebellion of Israel and their murder of the prophets and to the more recent destruction of Jerusalem in A.D. 70. The appending of the incident of the ill-clad guest was Matthew's warning to the Christian community, lest they fall away. In short, a simple story of a startling reversal of expectations has been moralized by Luke and Thomas to present an example, and allegorized by Matthew to offer an account of salvation history.

Summarizing to this point, Crossan asserts that the essence of Jesus' parables is a disrupting word which subverts the religious world-taken-for-granted and that the heart of all parables is paradox. For him, moreover, this has become the clue not only to the correct reading of the parables but also to a true understanding of the whole New Testament. The "parabolic" has been universalized, becoming the heart of the Christian message. Thus he can apply this perspective to other forms of Jesus' teaching and finally to Jesus himself.

In *Raid on the Articulate*, for example, it is argued that Jesus adopted this attitude towards the legal and sapiential traditions of Israel, even using parodies of their customary teaching forms to achieve his disruptive purpose. Case law is a major form of legal instruction in the Old Testament (if . . . then . . .). Matt. 5:39-41 records three sayings that are related to this. If you are struck on the right cheek, turn the other; if your coat is taken, offer also your cloak; if compelled to go a mile, go two. Luke 6:29 omits the last. Here again Crossan sees evidence of the attempt within tradition to soften the impact of Jesus' words by turning them into moral instruction concerning almsgiving and the non-resistance of evil. Matthew modifies the second so that violent theft becomes legal action ("sue you and take your coat"); Luke changes "right cheek" to "cheek" since presumably a right hand blow to the right cheek would have to be backhanded and thus more insulting. He omits entirely the hardest example of all, that calling for greater service to foreign soldiers who could require someone to carry their burdens one mile. Left in the original and startling form, the interpretation of such sayings as of God."[28] The supreme expression of that parabolic nature is the Cross. The Crucifixion seemed at first some terrible divine punishment of Jesus. In the light of his parabolic vision, however, it was no longer the rejection of all his claims but itself the "great Parable of God." So Paul could write to the Corinthians: "we preach Christ crucified, a stumbling-block to the Jews and folly to the Gentiles but [to us] ... the power of God and the wisdom of God" (I Cor. 1:23-24). While the evangelists so often softened the startling nature of Jesus' teachings, thus losing their parabolic impact, the basic preaching of the crucified Christ remained itself the disrupting Word of God, and thus the essence of the faith was preserved. Still the temptation to remove the foolishness of the gospel remains.

The crucial difference between religions, Crossan maintains, should not be seen in the often cited contrast between historical and mythical (or philosophical) religions; instead, the difference lies in the contrast between mythical and parabolic religion, between "a religion that gives one the final word about 'reality' and thereby excludes the authentic experience of mystery, and ... a religion that continually and deliberately subverts final words about 'reality' and thereby introduces the possibility of transcendence."[29] But with this we move beyond purely New Testament study to Crossan's basic vision of the nature of God and our ability to conceive of the divine.

A Philosophical/Theological Critique

Let us first examine this discussion of parables in terms of its implications for human understanding or, more precisely, for the limits of human understanding. In its initial phases Crossan's work presented basically a New Testament study focusing upon the teachings of Jesus, especially the parables. With the passage of time, it has become a metaphysical and epistemological vision. To grasp fully the impact of his conclusions concerning the New Testament, one must understand his philosophical position as well.

At a first level, Crossan merely echoes the traditional, biblical assertion that God is above and beyond our finite, human, intellectual capacities. God is mystery and we misperceive the divine if, in Marcel's terms, we replace that mystery with a problem that we presume to solve to some degree. Beginning in his first work, *In Parables,* he reminds us that God is transcendent, "the Wholly

---

28 Crossan, *The Dark Interval*, p. 124.
29 Ibid., p. 128

Other," and as such escapes human language and thought. The divine cannot be captured by our imagination and conceptualizations. It is "permanently and not just temporarily inexpressible.... Here it is not a question even of imagining at the limits of one's imagination but rather of imagining wholly new ways of imagining."[30] In *Raid on the Articulate* he addresses this issue in terms of the Old Testament prohibition against graven images, which for him involves more than merely rejecting graphic representations of the divine. Even language can be a falsifying trap if we believe that with it we can catch the divine nature. Therefore the iconoclasm of the Old Testament must also be applied to verbal images, to language. In religious terms, we must be alert to the idolatrous potential of our theologies. Thus far Crossan remains well within biblical tradition, but we have yet to encounter the major philosophical and theological import of his work.

At the heart of Crossan's evolving position is a very powerful, epistemological claim with an associated metaphysical vision. These carry us beyond the necessary corollaries of the biblical witness, although one might debate whether or not they contradict that witness. At the purely epistemological level, he denies the possibility of objective knowledge of reality. In the case of God, this becomes a denial of all knowledge in the sense of any positive content. At a metaphysical level, he gives serious consideration to the possibility that this may be so because "objective reality" has no fixed nature to be known or, indeed, may even be said not to exist at all. Applying such thought to God, he can write: "The Holy has no ... plan at all and that is what is absolutely incomprehensible to our structuring human minds.... [This] represents my own position."[31]

The dominant epistemology guiding Western culture for three centuries has assumed that sensory experience is fixed and neutral, and that theories are human interpretations of such data. Against this, Crossan refers to the growing conviction that all data is theory-laden, citing Karl Popper and Mary Hesse, both of whom reject the possibility of objective knowledge.

> "Reality" is the world we create in and by our language and our story so that what is "out there," apart from our imagination and without our language, is ... unknowable.... I am not saying we cannot know reality. I am claiming that what we know *is* reality, *is* our reality here together and with each other.[32]

30 Crossan, *In Parables*, pp. 13-14.
31 Crossan, *Raid on the Articulate*, p. 44. Cf. *In Parables*, p. 31.
32 Crossan, *The Dark Interval*, p. 40 (his emphasis).

This is more than the repudiation of objective knowledge, however; it is a rejection of any real knowledge of the world or of God, a claim going beyond Popper and Hesse. The position is stated more strongly in *Raid on the Articulate* where it is the core of the whole argument:

> I am presuming in all this that it is the playful human mind which establishes and imposes structure. I do not think of structures as already existent in "reality-out-there" and discovered or acknowledged by our obedient minds. What is there before or without our structured play strikes me as being both unknowable and unspeakable.[33]

Here is the temptation of language, the idolatrous side of theology. As the highest form of human play, language can deceive us into thinking that it indeed has *captured* a reality-out-there when we should be acknowledging that it has in fact *created* that reality. Human conceptualization, human knowledge, offer no real insight into the *extra nos*; rather "we are making it all up in the supreme game of language."[34] But surely at that level, then, our epistemological finitude applies not only to God but to all referential language as well. We cannot even know rocks, trees, or our neighbour!

In the opening pages of *The Dark Interval*, Crossan focuses upon the problem of objective knowledge. All our conceptions of what we assume to be an *extra nos* reality are coloured by individual and societal pre-understandings. In his terms, we comprehend everything from within our story. Thus we cannot approach the divine with a naked mind, free from all determining preconceptions, any more than we can approach nature that way. So what about theology? If there is only story, then God (the Transcendent) is either within the story, and thus a creation of the human imagination and for biblical faith an idol, or outside the story, and hence unknowable. We end with a negative epistemology, with a denial of any knowledge of the Wholly Other.

Yet Crossan is unwilling to rest here with a kind of cognitive death of God. Rather, his purpose, as already indicated, is to prepare the way for an experience of God, for a "renewal of transcendence." So he tells a story; he paints a picture. Imagine a group of people at sea on a raft while on shore there is a lighthouse with a lighthouse keeper. Even when those on the raft are lost on the tossing sea, they are confident that the lighthouse keeper knows where they are and

---

33 Crossan, *Raid on the Articulate*, p. 34.
34 Ibid., p. 93.

can guide them. For many, such is an image of reality. God is the lighthouse keeper and whatever our doubts about human understanding, God knows the truth. Now just suppose that Nietzsche is correct, that there is no lighthouse keeper, that even the concept of God is a product of our imagination. Obviously, "the fixed center outside language" would be gone and for many "that could only mean the burial of God since they equated the two."[35] For Crossan, however, such an epistemological death of God does not entail an ontological one. The very existence of limits can become an experience (even if ineffable) of the transcendent we have called God. In the language of his story, Crossan remarks, "We cannot really talk of the sea, we can only talk of the edges of the raft and what happens there. Our prayer will have to be, not 'Thank God for edges,' but 'Thank edges for God.'"[36] This very experience of limitation, ignorance, and uncertainty becomes the moment of true encounter with the divine.

Given this epistemological and metaphysical vision, Crossan's predilection to emphasize the disruptive as the religiously significant word becomes readily understandable. If the truth is that we cannot know the truth, then the saving word is iconoclastic. Throughout his writings our attention is frequently directed to paradox, which is seen as the literary device that confronts us with the inadequacy of all human understanding. Jesus "announces God as the shatterer of world, as the One of permanent eschatology, and so his language is sharpened necessarily into paradox, for paradox is to language as eschaton is to world."[37] Only the language of paradox is adequate to convey the truth that we do not know the truth. Thus paradox, especially in the narrative form of parable, was the major teaching style of Jesus. Parables serve "an epistemology of loss" and thereby "give God room."[38]

> They are stories which shatter the deep structure of our accepted world and thereby render clear and evident to us the relativity of story itself. They remove our defences and make us vulnerable to God. It is only in such experiences that God can touch us, and only in such moments does the kingdom of God arrive.[39]

Crossan's emphasis upon the disruptive word flows naturally from this philosophical position and particularly from its stark epis-

35 Crossan, *The Dark Interval*, p. 43.
36 Ibid., p. 45.
37 Crossan, *In Parables*, p. 76.
38 Crossan, *The Dark Interval*, pp. 77, 121.
39 Ibid., p. 122.

temology. The religious genius of Jesus and his investment in parabolic language presumably are the consequence of his awareness of the failure of all human conceptualizations. Yet is this view of human understanding as obvious and convincing as Crossan seems to believe? The first phase of his argument seems very persuasive. There is no such thing as "objective" knowledge. The results of modern philosophy, sociology, and psychology agree in rejecting such naive claims to unbiased cognition. But does this necessarily entail the denial of all cognition per se, all knowledge of the *extra nos*? There is a radical difference between saying that we possess no neutral, unbiased knowledge, no concepts which are not shaped by our pre-understanding and our limited range of sensa, and saying that we possess no knowledge whatsoever of the other. Popper and Hesse agree that all models of reality are theory and culture-laden. In that sense " 'reality' is the world we create in and by our language."[40] Applying this to theology, we can say that "the Christian myth . . . is no more and no less than just that—a magnificent construct of the human imagination."[41] But the denial of "objective" truth did not cause either Popper or Hesse to regard science as a language game that provides no meaningful insight into the *extra nos*. The rejection of simplistic concepts of unbiased truth does not require the rejection of all truth concerning reality out there. In *The Dark Interval* Crossan moves quickly from the thought of Popper and Hesse to the assertion of the subjective dimensions of awareness, and thence to the denial of the possibility of any knowledge of God. What Crossan does not acknowledge as immediately is that his argument (if correct) would hold for all thought, including his own theory about knowing. Simply because my conception of the other is admittedly influenced by subjective or personal factors does not mean that I am left with no valid awareness of it. Such a conclusion stands against common sense in the best meaning of that phrase.

    We know rocks, trees, and our neighbour because we encounter them. But Crossan allows that we also encounter God at the edges of life, "a God who is not just our projected vanity."[42] Surely if we encounter the Transcendent, however, if we enter into relationships, our perceptions of that Other have the potential to be shaped in a true fashion by it, or else we grant to the Divine less ontological reality than we do to rocks, trees, and neighbours. In short, though all knowledge

40 Ibid., p. 40.
41 Crossan, *Raid on the Articulate*, p. 137.
42 Ibid., p. 174.

of God is imperfect and the denial of this amounts to worshipping theologies spun within our own imaginations, it does not follow that such imagining is in no way responsive to and therefore shaped by the Divine, that God-concepts are simply a product of play. Moreover, if God is indeed encountered, if at the edges of life we do respond and gain insight into the Transcendent, on what basis do we restrict that encounter to life's boundaries? Why not, in Tillich's phrase, at its depths? In summary, while the disruptive note is a necessary caveat in theology (indeed in all human understanding), it is not the only word. Language can also convey, however imperfectly, some true insight into the *extra nos*. Theology is not reduced to a *via negativa* alone. If the teachings of Jesus amount only to paradox and disruption, if we are to understand Christ solely in terms of the parabolic, then the message of the New Testament would appear to be wanting and markedly incomplete. It is hardly a cause to claim some superiority. My purpose is not to defend theology's cognitive claims, since I have already attempted this elsewhere.[43] It is sufficient here to establish that the epistemology assumed by Crossan creates a bias towards the parabolic as the true word. One cannot but feel that his "discovery" of the primacy of the disruptive in Jesus is in part a product of his pre-understanding.

Yet Crossan appears to be making more than these epistemological claims; he proffers a metaphysical vision as well and one which, as I have indicated, questions the very existence of any ordered reality beyond or apart from human imagination. "There is no objective order except language itself."[44] "My suspicion is that existential absurdity or absurd existentialism is but the dull receding roar of rationalism. Why should it be deemed absurd that what was never there was never there? Comic, by all means, but absurd protests too much."[45] While affirming the importance of Crossan's work on the disruptive dynamic of parable, William Beardslee makes the interesting suggestion that we should see the parabolic moment as opening "the hearer to an experience of creative Nothing, the transcendent creativity which escapes all conceptualization."[46] The classic doctrine of the Trinity, he continues, is an attempt to express a pluralistic understanding of the Transcendent but it fails to include the experi-

---

43 John C. Hoffman, "On Theology's Cognitive Claims: A. J. Ayer Revisited," *Studies in Religion* 6:2 (1976-77), pp. 117-26.
44 Crossan, *Raid on the Articulate*, p. 180.
45 Ibid., p. 18.
46 William Beardslee, "Parable, Proverb, and Koan," *Semeia* 12 (1978), p. 168.

ence of it as "pure creative negativity."[47] The parabolic experience in this case would itself become an expression of content. He feels that the recent work of John Cobb, which compares Christian and Buddhist images of the divine and results in an attempt to develop a model of the Godhead that includes both the conceptual content of the traditional Christian image and the creative emptiness of Buddhist expression, catches something of this expanded view wherein parable's disruptive impact is itself a kind of affirmation.

Our discussion to this point has highlighted the basic epistemological issues concerning the possibilities and limitations of human understanding, particularly of understanding deity. We need not accept Crossan's pessimistic vision, which would appear to preclude all but a negative awareness of God and to rule out the validity of substantive content in theology, to recognize the claim that all religious truth must carry the caveat of imperfection, that it has not in fact captured the divine nature. God transcends our theologies. Thus, an important aspect of theological assertions must be the inclusion of a warning against taking them with final certainty. Without this, theological assertions may actually convey falsehood in the expression of truth. In terms which we shall develop later, a theological structure or nomos needs to carry a lively sense of the transnomic.

A Literary/Phenomenological Critique

Let us turn finally to a discussion of the light the study of parables and Crossan throws upon the hearing and telling of stories. What is revealed concerning the dynamics of narrative experience?

Contemporary New Testament studies exhibit a growing interest in literary criticism as a necessary addition to past emphases on historical criticism. In brief, literary critics argue that form and content cannot be separated. An author's choice of drama, lyric poem, or novel to convey meaning is inevitably part of the meaning conveyed. Such critics take seriously the literary forms employed in the New Testament.

In developing his thesis, Crossan offers a functional definition of five literary types. "Myth establishes world. Apologue defends world. Action investigates world. Satire attacks world. Parable subverts world."[48] This functional emphasis is dominant in his work, especially in the connotation given to the term "parable." *In Parables* speaks of

47 Ibid., p. 169.
48 Crossan, *The Dark Interval*, p. 59.

permanent eschatology, of the continual shattering of one's world and of parables of reversal. *The Dark Interval* offers us parables under the heading "parables as contradiction." It finds the essence of such narratives to be the overthrow of expectations, the clash between the automatic assumptions of the listener and the design of the storyteller. Thus "one can tell oneself stories but not parables. One cannot really do so just as one cannot really beat oneself at chess or fool oneself completely with a riddle one has just invented. It takes two to parable."[49] *Raid on the Articulate* further expounds this disruptive function by defining parables as "paradoxes formed into a story by effecting single or double reversals of the audience's most profound expectations."[50] Given this functional emphasis, Crossan can refer to Jesus as the Great Parable and see his impact as one which subverts our religious worlds. He also emphasizes the functional in the definition of myth as a story by which people rehearse and celebrate ultimate meaning. Myth is reality-defining.

Myth, Crossan notes, has also been substantively defined as stories about gods and goddesses or primal ancestors, as tales that take place outside our time and space. Leaving aside the popular but technically incorrect usage which sees it as sophisticated lie, we run into difficulties when we seek an agreed-upon substantive definition of parable, but Crossan makes a passing attempt:

> A parable tells a story which, on its surface level, is absolutely possible or even factual within the normalcy of life. A myth tells one which is neither of these on its surface level. In parable one talks of the very road between Jerusalem and Jericho; in myth one talks of centaurs in a dragon world.[51]

To be complete, in these terms one needs to add a third category of narrative, one which is set in our world and time but which describes events transcending "the normalcy of life." These narratives, I suggest, have traditionally been called legends. Parables, then, would be all stories that are neither myths nor legends—a conception which does not define a very precise area. However, this itself is suggestive. Amos Wilder points out that the Old Testament antecedent of the parable, the *marshal*, was "first of all a comparison of some kind, but it included a wide variety of metaphors, similitudes, riddles, mysteries and illustrations."[52] He continues: "we may say that the term 'para-

---

49   Ibid., p. 87.
50   Crossan, *Raid on the Articulate*, p. 98.
51   Crossan, *In Parables*, p. 15.
52   Wilder, *Early Christian Rhetoric*, p. 72.

ble' is misleading since it suggests a single pattern and often distorts our understanding of this or that special case."[53]

Nevertheless, having recognized that stories can be defined either substantively or functionally, one immediately faces the possibility that the two definitions will not map out the same area. One can surely tell subverting stories about gods and goddesses and can define reality in a tale set within our space and time. The Exodus was the latter type of story for the Israelites: *The Plague*, pure fiction, may have been such for Camus. If we define a group of stories by some substantive definition, especially as broad as those told by Jesus, must we assume that they all fulfill the same function? Specifically, even if some are world-subverting, we need not assume all to be so. Thus, for example, some of Crossan's original parables of advent and parables of action, such as the parable of the Sower and the parable of the Talents, may well have been told to offer a religious vision and not merely to disrupt. Moreover, must we assume, as Crossan appears to do, that narratives necessarily have only one function? If the parable of the Good Samaritan is indeed intended to disrupt the complacency of our religious understanding, might it not also have other essential purposes even in the mind of Jesus?

In order to avoid confusion, I want now to distinguish two contrasting literary functions: the *mythic*, which defines reality, and the *parabolic*, which disrupts it. This is a contrast quite different than that between *parable* as a general class of religious stories, especially those told by Jesus, which—at least on the surface—describe ordinary events in our world, and *myth*, which is a story about gods or ancestors, occurring outside our space and/or time. It is probably correct to say that religions have generally told myths for mythic purposes. The point at issue becomes Crossan's claim that the parables of Jesus, as a class, were recounted for parabolic impact.

Crossan sets parable in three contrasts, with myth, with example story or apologue, and with anti-myth. In the terminology just set forth this amounts to a contrast between the parabolic and the mythic, the exemplifying, and the counter-mythic functions of narrative. The mythic and parabolic are united in addressing the depth dimension, in confronting the basic issue of ultimate meaning. They differ in that myth claims to convey such meaning, parable to subvert it. In contrast, an example story or apologue assumes meaning, lives with a world-taken-for-granted, and seeks to illustrate and defend it. Crossan also contrasts parable with anti-myth. The encounter with a

---

53 Ibid., p. 73.

radically different interpretation of life, a new religious vision, can be a profoundly disruptive experience. In the broadest sense of the term, it can be parabolic. The parabolic, in a more restricted way, however, does not present a competing world view but subverts all world views. It is this starker connotation of the term which underlies his assertion of the parabolic character of Jesus' message so that even the Christian world view is subverted thereby.

I have already presented philosophical reasons to challenge this stark opinion of human understanding and of Jesus' teachings. As Crossan admits, Christian tradition has not seen these teachings in such a light. Addressing himself specifically to Crossan, Amos Wilder asserts that his view "is congenial to our contemporary iconoclastic mysticism and thirst for the Absolute, but disengages Jesus too radically from his home soil and the faith of his fathers. Jesus' mythos of the kingdom of God has more content in it than this kind of ontological reversal."[54] I want now to approach this issue by examining the broader question of the nature of narrative experience. What is the effect (and therefore the function) of hearing a story? Are any stories, in fact, purely mythic or parabolic?

Here let me present a thesis concerning the nature of narrative experience, derived from this study of the parables, a thesis which I shall simply state now, and seek to support in the two subsequent chapters.

Clearly, stories define self and world for individuals and peoples. Crossan introduces his first study with a series of quotations including one by Hugh Kenner: "Whoever can give his people better stories than the ones they live in is like the priest in whose hands common bread and wine become capable of feeding the very soul, and he may think of forging in some invisible smithy the uncreated conscience of his race."[55] In the words of *The Dark Interval*, we all live in a story. There is no place else for us to be. But more than this, story is always a world. Language is the supreme act of human play whereby we create our world and the totality of meaning. This, of course, is Via's basic view, and so he asserts that "all literature contains *inherently*, even though implicitly and indirectly . . . a world view or understanding of existence."[56] And Amos Wilder contends:

> Any human language represents a special kind of order superimposed upon existence. Generations live in it as a habitat in which they

---

54 Amos N. Wilder, *Theopoetic* (Philadelphia: Fortress Press, 1976), p. 77.
55 Crossan, *In Parables*, p. 2.
56 Via, *The Parables*, p. 71 (his emphasis).

are born and die. Outside it is nescience. The language of a people is its fate. Thus the poets or seers who purify the language of a tribe are truly world-makers and the 'unacknowledged legislators of the world.'[57]

What all of this suggests, I believe, is that language—and especially, the hearing of stories—inevitably offers the listener a world in which to live. It is an invitation to experience reality from a particular perspective, to worship a certain god, to follow one way, to adopt heroes, to celebrate hope or sink in despair.[58] Whatever the primary intention of the narrator and whatever the dominant impact of the tale, to hear a story—any story—is to be offered a world in which to live or an account of life in an assumed world. All stories in this sense are either mythic or exemplifying. All offer some content for understanding, some picture of reality.

I feel that Crossan is correct in arguing that we miss the import of the story of the Good Samaritan if we fail to sense its disruptive character in calling a Samaritan "good." Yet here is more than the parabolic: there is content as well. He admits that "what the Samaritan does is a good action absolutely to be imitated."[59] This is not accidental exception. If for simplicity I may broaden the term to include all meaning or worlds in any sense, then all stories are mythic. That is the nature of the narrative experience. (It might be possible to offer a purely parabolic message. Such a case has been made for some of the sayings of Jesus. "Let the dead bury the dead." "To him who has will be given; and from him who has not will be taken away." Crossan refers to these as "paradoxical aphorisms."[60] Narrative, I stress, always carries the mythic.)

But now we must make the exactly opposite claim: all stories are parabolic. Insofar as they offer a new image of reality, an alternative understanding of experience, some stories can present an anti-myth and, in that sense, be parabolic. Other stories are primarily parabolic with a basic intent to challenge or disrupt a world-taken-for-granted without offering an alternative. Crossan and Via both see the message of Jesus as representing a profound challenge to the religious self-understanding of his audience. For Via, this was the disruptive impact of the anti-mythic. For Crossan, it was the shattering en-

57 Wilder, *Early Christian Rhetoric*, p. 5.
58 The experience of modern psychotherapy lends strong support to this contention that we understand ourselves by and live in stories.
59 Crossan, *In Parables*, p. 65.
60 Crossan, *Raid on the Articulate*, p. 70.

counter with the purely parabolic word which announces the advent of God but proclaims it as one "for which wise and prudent readiness is impossible because it shatters also our wisdom and our prudence."[61] Even such traditional interpreters of the New Testament as Via and Wilder allow for the purely parabolic in the teachings of Jesus, that is, for narrative elements which challenge and subvert without, at the same time, offering an alternative image. Sometimes they describe this as the "parabolic moment" in the appropriation of a story. For Via the jolt from the parable of the Workers in the Vineyard is of this character. Wilder and Via differ, however, in seeing the parabolic as subordinate to the mythic. Thus we may say that narrative experience includes hearing stories which disrupt either as anti-myth or as essentially parabolic. This is not true of all narrative, though, for the myth and apologue were written not to disrupt or challenge the faith, but to defend it. While some of the legends of the saints may clash with our modern world view, to the pious of the Middle Ages they were simply a picture of how things were or a model for their own lives, possibly a portrait of a hero to be imitated. They found nothing parabolic there.

Nevertheless, I believe that all stories contain a parabolic dimension because of the way they invite the listener's participation. They encourage us to enter their world, to encounter new people and events where, especially in the presence of a good storyteller, we are lifted out of ourselves and our setting. For a moment we experience another perspective, another possibility which in itself reminds us that ours is not the only one. The middle-class white person may momentarily feel what it is to be a black person in the ghettos of New York or an Inuit in the Canadian North. Moreover, even when it is our story in our world and in no sense anti-myth, narrative can ignite the imagination. (Perhaps the real death of God and the power of the enslaving iron cage lie in a failure of this liberating imagination.) We are enabled to dream dreams, imagine new possibilities, try new roles, dare to be different. Best of all, stories awaken the child in us; they awaken wonder, fantasy, and play. They free our capacity to "sit loose" to the whole things, to restore the world *sub specie ludi*. Yet, contrary to what Crossan seems to imply, this inevitable parabolic dimension does not declare reality as the mere play of the imagination, and the only true word as parabolic. Rather, it reminds us that to know reality we must play with it. We must remember that truth comes not from holding fast to our own conceptions with deadly earnestness, but

---

61 Crossan, *In Parables*, p. 120.

through continuing to seek new understanding and holding no idea or thought beyond question. We must continue to interact with the *extra nos* in the dance of life.

Inevitably, then, story offers us a world to live in, an understanding of existence, and yet invites us to play with that world, liberating our own imaginations and retelling the story in a new way. By its very nature, narrative experience, including the parables of Jesus as heard by the crowds or read today, is at once mythic *and* parabolic or, better still, *mythoparabolic*. In the moment of the storyteller the apparent poles meet. Thus, while Jesus may have told the story of the Good Samaritan to challenge the religious prejudices of his day, it was an inevitable part of this whole experience—not a falsification of the message—to hear it also as an example story. Conversely, while the Hebrews told the story of the Exodus mythically, to affirm their faith in a providential God of history, it is fully congruent with its truth for us to have Third World theologians disrupt our complacency by inviting us to consider that we are the Egyptians and not the Israelites. Similarly, feminist theologians may retell the story of Abraham and the "sacrifice" of Isaac, requesting that we see it through Sarah's eyes.

Paul Tillich asserted that vital religion requires both the "Protestant principle," which warns that "no man can boast about his grasp of God," and "Catholic substance, the concrete embodiment of Spiritual Presence."[62] In terms of our literary types, we require both parabolic challenge and mythic affirmation. Crossan suggests that "the world needs a few less heroes and a few more fools,"[63] a few less models offered as the way and a few more jesters to prick the pretensions of models and worlds. But surely we need heroes as well as fools and, because it offers a mythoparabolic experience, narrative can supply both. Crossan has significantly enriched our view of the New Testament by highlighting the parabolic element in the teachings of Jesus. Given the dual potential of story, however, I believe it is to misread or *under*read the parables if we assume that they offer only that. Moreover, because of their mythoparabolic character, stories are perhaps the most effective witness to the Ultimate, which may well be both the Triune God of traditional conceptualization and the Creative Emptiness transcending all conceptualization.

In summary, this study of the parables and the work of John Crossan has raised two issues. Crossan supports a negative judgment

62 Paul Tillich, *Systematic Theology*, vol. 3 (Chicago: University of Chicago Press, 1963), p. 245.
63 Crossan, *Raid on the Articulate*, p. 11.

of our ability to conceive of ultimate or divine realities. He offers what I have called the epistemological death of God, a radical iconoclasm of all theological language. While not accepting this extreme posture, we recognize the validity of his emphasis upon the limitations of all religious claims, the need to accompany doctrine with this clear warning: "Not to be taken with absolute certainty." (This is a subject I shall take up again in the fifth chapter.) Moreover, we have suggested that the very character of narrative experience inevitably offers a world in which to live, a guiding framework for at least some aspects of life. We have seen that the great religious myths captured the basic assumptions and value judgments of a people, in terms of which they answered their questions concerning ultimate truth, beauty, and goodness. Even stories which disrupt a world-take-for-granted always carry with that disruption at least a partial image of another world. Yet as long as stories remain alive as stories, even those basically mythic stories, by awaking our playful fantasy and participation, they foster a degree of freedom with which to transcend, challenge, and disrupt the very worlds they offer. It is these insights and their relationship to each other, but especially what I have called the mythoparabolic character of stories that I will now pursue further by examining narrative experience in therapy and social process.

3
Story and Fantasy in Psychotherapy

Frederick Streng has defined religion as "a means of ultimate transformation,"[1] drawing attention to religion not only as a body of doctrine or a set of rituals but as a change agent. In a similar vein, Peter Slater speaks of religion as "a personal way of life... directed toward the realization of some transcendent end,"[2] and Aarne Siirala calls for theology to help articulate "a language of healing and transformation."[3] We have already discussed the powerful place of story in religious traditions: myths of creation, legendary accounts of founders and heroes, teaching stories. Given these factors, it is natural to inquire into the possible function of storytelling as a means of transformation. It is with this interest that we now move to the field of psychotherapy.

The twentieth century has witnessed the dramatic development of a major mode of human transformation, namely psychotherapy. Following the work of Sigmund Freud came a proliferation of diverse

1 Frederick J. Streng, *Understanding Religious Man* (Belmont, California: Dickenson Publishing, 1969), p. 4.
2 Peter Slater, *The Dynamics of Religion* (New York: Harper and Row, 1978), p. 6.
3 Aarne Siirala, "Theology and the Unconscious," *Studies in Religion* 6:6 (1976-77), p. 622.

schools, at times with quite radically contrasting assumptions concerning human nature, but all dedicated to the healing of individuals plagued with psychic distress. While we may, of course, dispute the interpretation of psychic health and disease assumed in some schools, there is no doubt that the general field of psychotherapy has been effective in assisting men and women in finding greater peace, stability, and cohesion in their lives. Thus the study of religion turns to examine the uses of story in psychotherapy to see what light this throws upon the place of narrative in religion. It becomes a particularly compelling area for investigation in view of such dramatic claims as James Hillman's: "From my perspective as depth psychologist, I see that those who have a connection with story are in better shape and have a better prognosis than those to whom story must be introduced. . . . To have 'story-awareness' is *per se* psychologically therapeutic."[4] One naturally asks whether such awareness is also spiritually therapeutic, and if so, what are its implications for the task and style of theology.

The Narrative Character of Self-Understanding

The direct use of story, and especially of fantasy, in psychotherapy has really only developed in the last thirty years. Before that, however, narrative had found a place in the emerging agreement that the individual's sense of identity could be said to take the form of a personal biography.

Patients' problems arise from their mode of interpreting reality, which either distorts their experience or unnecessarily limits their options in responding to their situation. The difficulty is "in their *representation* of the world and not in the world itself."[5] While various metaphors have been employed in discussing representational systems, from the earliest expressions of modern psychotherapy such outlooks have tended to be seen as the result of personal experiences, which affect our lives in the form of conscious and unconscious memories. Given the focus of therapy, interest was directed to those past experiences or memories that resulted in

---

4   James Hillman, *Loose Ends* (Zurich: Spring Publications, 1975), p. 1.
5   John Grinder and Richard Bandler, *The Structure of Magic*, vol. 2 (Palo Alto: Science and Behavior Books, 1976), p. 3 (their emphasis). To be sure, this type of assumption gives some justification to the concern among ethicists that therapy has tended to be too conservative, fostering adjustment rather than social reform.

dysfunctional representational systems, leading to some form of psychopathology. In his first work with Josef Breuer, Freud was drawn to the lasting effects of what he presumed to be memories of actual experiences. *"Our hysterical patients suffer from reminiscences. Their symptoms are the remnants and the memory symbols of certain (traumatic) experiences."*[6] So a young woman suffers from hydrophobia, leading to a tormenting thirst, as a result of a childhood experience in which she saw her governess giving her loathsome dog a drink from a glass. (Not all of Freud's traumas were sexual.) We have, in effect, a formative experience which continues to operate, shaping a whole series of subsequent moments and behaviours in the individual's life. Later, Freud came to suspect that many of these reported traumas were matters of fantasy, not history, but whether history or fantasy, the results were the same. "In contrast to *material* reality these phantasies possess *psychical* reality, and we gradually come to understand that *in the world of neurosis PSYCHICAL REALITY is the determining factor.*"[7] It is not, then, simply objective, historical experience which sets up a pattern of behaviour, a mode of interpreting and responding to reality, but one's subjective experience, including the most fanciful interpretations of actual events.

Psychopathology is sustained by the absence of awareness of these formative impressions which play a determinative role in the present, thus precluding any re-evaluation of childhood judgments and reactions. Therapy consists in the lifting of amnesia of childhood. "When all gaps in memory have been filled in, all the enigmatic products of mental life elucidated, the continuance and even the renewal of the morbid condition is impossible."[8] At first Freud thought of this as a purely cognitive matter. The therapist gained insight into the forgotten experiences and shared this with the patient. Yet even in the 1890s Freud reported instances of what he described as a "counter-will" in which the patient seemed to fight against receiving the healing insight. Freud found, for example, that when he was able to gain knowledge of the formative incident from external sources—parents, nurses, friends—simply conveying this information to the patient did not bring healing but often intensified resistance. An intellectualist view of the situation was clearly inadequate. It

---

6 Sigmund Freud, *The Origin and Development of Psychoanalysis* (Chicago: Gateway Edition, 1955), p. 11 (his emphasis).

7 Sigmund Freud, *A General Introduction to Psychoanalysis* (New York: Washington Square Press, 1960), p. 378 (his emphasis).

8 Sigmund Freud, "Freud's Psycho-analytic Method," *Collected Papers*, vol. 1 (London: The Hogarth Press, 1924), p. 269.

was not enough to pass on objective data concerning the patient's unconscious feelings about some person or incident. Healing required reliving and working through the traumatic past in the therapeutic relationship. "Finally every conflict has to be fought out in the sphere of transference."[9] It is not, then, merely the past as some objective set of facts, or even facts about the nature of early emotional reactions and fantasies, that is significant; rather, it is that experience as emotionally accepted and consciously recognized. Patients continue exhibiting neurotic behaviours because of the influence of unconscious memories of events, real or imagined, which they accept as reality-defining. We have, then, the dual distinctions between conscious and unconscious memories, and between history as observed, *Historie*, and history as experiences, *Geschichte*. Freud went on to develop the determinative role of the primal family. Psychic health requires a creative resolution of the inevitable Oedipal conflict. (In light of a discussion later in this chapter, it is noteworthy that he chose to portray this situation by appealing to a Greek myth.)

Much in keeping with the feelings of Freud concerning the past, but not with his emphasis on sexual etiology, is the work of Alfred Adler.

> The greatest of all helps, however, in gaining a quick comprehension of the meaning an individual gives to himself and to life comes through his memories. Every memory, however trivial he may think it, represents to him something *memorable*. It is memorable because of its bearing on life as he pictures it. . . . The memories of early childhood are especially useful in showing how long standing is the individual's own peculiar approach to life, and in giving the circumstances in which he first crystallized his life-attitude.[10]

Adler went on to emphasize that as one alters one's style of life, memories change also. Whether the result of the intervention of a therapist or the impact of contemporary experiences, a change in one's basic understandings of self and the world that produces a fundamental shift in lifestyle is associated with a modification in the memories which are a vehicle for that understanding. Memories, *Geschichten*, are inevitably syntonic with lifestyle and behaviour. The novel *The Pawnbroker* reflects this syntonic relationship as it tells of a survivor of the death camp, obsessed with dreams and

9 Sigmund Freud, quoted in Reuben Fine, *Freud, A Critical Re-evaluation of his Theories* (New York: David McKay, 1962), p. 100.
10 Alfred Adler, *What Life Should Mean to You* (New York: Capricorn Books, 1958), p. 19.

memories of its horrors, who protects himself from further pain by refusing to have a close, caring relationship with anyone. When at last a social worker breaks through his defenses and he risks a relationship, he begins to remember happy times before the war. Again, like Freud, Adler stresses the internal images, the pictures we relive of the past. "It is comparatively indifferent whether the memories are accurate or inaccurate; what is of most value about them is that they represent the individual's judgment, 'Even in childhood, I was such and such a person. . . .'"[11]

We all know that there are major differences among the various schools of psychotherapy in basic assumptions concerning human nature. Transactional analysis represents one of the more popular and more optimistic schools that fall within the larger classification of humanistic therapies and stand in sharp contrast to Freud's anthropology of conflict. In his characteristically picturesque language, Eric Berne, the founder of transactional analysis, asserted: "People are born princes and princesses, until their parents turn them into frogs."[12] Berne initiated the use of a variety of everyday terms to identify psychiatric realities. Particular neurotic or dysfunctional behaviour patterns he called "games" and the constellation of games or behaviours which make up one's lifestyle he termed a "script." "Script theory is based on the belief that people make conscious life plans in childhood or early adolescence which influence and make predictable the rest of their lives."[13] As Berne stressed, these life plan decisions are "reinforced by the parents, and justified by subsequent events."[14] Children make basic decisions, amounting to interpretations of life and behaviour within the primal family context, and these set the pattern for their fundamental orientation to life from that point on, a pattern which operates successfully, albeit at a cost, in the sense that it is reinforced by subsequent events. The term "script" carries not only a dramatic or narrative flavour but also the sense of a self-fulfilling prophecy: "This is the life I will inevitably lead." Scripts may be compared to repetition compulsion in psychoanalytic theory. Indeed, it is this note that transactional analysts pick up in the Oedipus myth. For them *Oedipus Rex* echoes, not with the sense of sexual passion, but with the spectators' "realization of their own

11 Ibid., p. 75.
12 Eric Berne, quoted in Claude M. Steiner, *Scripts People Live* (New York: Grove Press, 1974), p. 2.
13 Steiner, *Scripts People Live*, p. 23.
14 Eric Berne, *Beyond Games and Scripts* (New York: Grove Press, 1976), p. 350.

impotence in the face of fate."[15] Therapy's aim is to break this sense of impotence, to disrupt the tragic script of the woman who marries one alcoholic after another, or in Berne's characteristic language style, "to close the show and put a better one on the road."[16] Adopting the language focus of this study, we could say that this means to choose to understand oneself and live according to a different story.

One notes, in passing, other parallels with the earlier depth psychologies. Particular prominence is given to the importance of childhood experiences and feelings in setting the character of life dramas. Recognition is granted as well to the role of shared or cultural scripting, patterning behaviour in a manner reminiscent of the work of Erik Erikson on cultural identity. Once more, healing involves overcoming the amnesia of childhood. "The current life drama must then be related to its historical origins so that control of the individual's destiny can be shifted from the Child to the Adult, from archaeopsychic unconsciousness to neopsychic awareness."[17] Thus, a variant of transactional analysis, called "redecision therapy," emphasizes the need to "give up the constricting decisions ... made in childhood," and to make "a new decision—to overrule the pathological adaptation and function freely."[18] One chooses a new script, a new interpretation of life, a new story. Carl and Stephanie Simonton have employed a very similar framework, using psychotherapeutic techniques in the treatment of physical disease, especially cancer.[19] They too speak of the limitations of a person's resources for coping with stress, limitations that reflect childhood decisions, and they describe major physical improvements that result from making conscious these choices and from redeciding.

This whole process of becoming aware of our personal history (autobiography), and of its import for our lives, has become a highly developed art in the recent work of Ira Progoff who introduced the intensive journal technique. In essence, Progoff begins with objective historical accounts, with *Historie*, in the form of "stepping stones," a list of ten or twelve events leading up to the present and related to some element of one's life. Reflection upon such events in depth, by

15 Steiner, *Scripts People Live*, p. 54.
16 Berne, *Beyond Games and Scripts*, p. 128.
17 Ibid., p. 127. Berne, too, could use rather arcane language.
18 Mary and Robert Goulding, *Changing Lives Through Redecision Therapy* (New York: Brunner Mazel Publishers, 1979), pp. 9, 19.
19 O. Carl Simonton, Stephanie Matthews Simonton, and James Creighton, *Getting Well Again* (Los Angeles: J. P. Tarcher, 1978), passim.

means of various techniques, leads to a sense of their personal significance, a transformation of *Historie* into *Geschichte*. All this is done so that individuals might gain greater self-awareness and, thereafter, greater freedom. One recovers the past to be free in the present to plan the future.

> Working in our life history is progressive. Its cumulative effect is to draw our life into focus so that we have a basis for making decisions that are pressing at the moment, and also to give us a perspective of the pattern and context of our life as a whole. We work in our life history not because it contains our past experiences, but because our life history is our unique life story, and it is continuing to unfold in our present experiences. Working in it by means of our Journal experiences enables us to have an inner perspective of the movement of our life, and thus we can eventually have a dialogue relationship with our future.[20]

Progoff also notes that as persons undergo significant changes in their lifestyle they develop new lists of stepping stones with regard to the issue being explored. They become new people with different life histories than before.

Storytelling is not necessarily involved in these therapies, yet there is a developing sense that the patients understand themselves in terms of the story they have to tell. James Hillman suggests that "[s]ome of the healing that goes on in psychotherapy, maybe even the essence of it, is this collaborative fiction, this putting all the chaotic and traumatic events of a life into a new story."[21] As we move on now to more direct uses of story in treatment, one can argue that its effectiveness is related—in part—to this natural mode of self-understanding, or to what Stephen Crites calls "the narrative quality of experience."

Initially, the psychotherapeutic movement was not noted for the telling of stories. Indeed, in spite of the deep involvement with patients, it was characterized by a rather detached and prosaic tone. One pictures classical psychoanalysis with the therapist in the background, silently copying down the patient's words and speaking only enough to encourage continuation, or the Rogerian counselor, mirroring the client's thoughts. But within the rich diversity that marks the modern movement, one finds the growth of narrative modes in therapy. I have in mind two in particular: the actual telling of stories by

---

20   Ira Progoff, *At a Journal Workshop* (New York: Dialogue House Library, 1975), pp. 98-99.
21   Hillman, *Loose Ends*, p. 2.

the therapist, the patient, or both, and the use of imagination and fantasy as a therapeutic technique in individual and group settings.

The Telling of Stories

Prior to the actual introduction of storytelling as a therapeutic tool was the recognition among therapists that many traditional stories contain important psychological insights. One might say that the first person to note this was Freud himself when he saw in *Oedipus Rex* a dramatic expression of the primary struggles at the heart of human psychic development. Let us note that subsequent therapists have also seen significant psychological insights in this Greek classic, insights other than those that Freud claimed. The tragedy of Oedipus lends itself to several creative interpretations with therapeutic import. Such diversity of interpretation may suggest part of the healing power of story, namely, its rich openness to convey multiple levels of meaning.

Bruno Bettelheim's *The Uses of Enchantment* gives contemporary expression to the conviction that narrative is a vehicle for deep insights. Because of his interest in child therapy, Bettelheim is particularly drawn to fairy tales. "Though the fairy tale offers fantastic symbolic images for the solution of problems, the problems presented in them are ordinary ones: a child's suffering, from jealousy and discrimination of his siblings, as is true for Cinderella [for example]."[22] While Bettelheim recognizes that such stories may properly be explored from sociological, cultural, and religious perspectives, in keeping with his psychoanalytic posture he tends to think of them offering information, not so much about the external world as about the interior life of the child. Thus Little Red Riding Hood (or Little Red Cap) speaks of more than the dangers of trusting everyone:

> the wolf is not just the male seducer, he also represents all the asocial, animalistic tendencies within ourselves. By giving up the school-age child's virtues of "walking single-mindedly," as her task demands, Little Red Cap reverts to the pleasure-seeking oedipal child. . . . Only adults who are convinced that fairy stories do not make sense can fail to see that Little Red Cap's unconscious is working overtime to give Grandmother away.[23]

---

22 Bruno Bettelheim, *The Uses of Enchantment* (New York: Vintage Books, 1977), p. 40.
23 Ibid., pp. 172-73.

Judith R. Brown, in contrast, tends to treat stories entirely on the obvious, ordinary level as dramatic models of marital dynamics and patterns. The fact remains that stories do more than entertain; they inform us about life. All this, of course, would come as no surprise to the great figures of world literature. The Shakespeares, Goethes, and Dostoevskys have always known that they were capturing in dramatic form the deepest understandings of the human situation. Therapists have simply concentrated on one element of that meaning, the psychodynamic, which they have found to be effectively transmitted in a wide range of traditional literature.

Given the narrative character of self-understanding and the human experiential meaning expressed in literature, it is not surprising that a developed sense of narrative can be psychologically creative. As we shall see, this entails cultivating the imaginative side of the personality. More immediately, however, stories offer "a form of vicarious experience which can help people to see themselves, to extend horizons in empathy with those different from themselves and to contemplate and plan for their actions should *they* be faced with the same situation."[24] As Hillman puts it, "One integrates life as a story because one has stories in the back of the mind (unconscious) as containers for organizing events into meaningful experiences. The stories are means of telling oneself into events that might not otherwise make psychological sense at all."[25] Joanne E. Bernstein has proposed a bibliotherapeutic approach to grief work with children. While providing a suitable supply of stories about death does not preclude the need to be available for discussion, nonetheless, "through literature, children can see that they are not alone in their reactions to problems. The opportunity to identify with characters and, subsequently, to discuss feelings is presented in gentle, subtle form. Books can be the catalysts for spontaneous release of previously hidden emotions."[26] In this connection Bettelheim laments the "prettified and simplified versions" of fairy tales in modern film and TV that rob these stories of their therapeutic power and turn them into "empty-minded entertainment."[27] Stories are potentially therapeutic because in dramatic form they capture basic insights into human existence and models for human behaviour.

24 Joanne Bernstein, "Helping Young Children to Cope with Acute Grief: A Bibliotherapy Approach," in Vanderlyn R. Pine et al. (eds.), *Acute Grief and the Funeral* (Springfield, Ill.: C. C. Thomas Publishers, 1976), p. 274.
25 Hillman, *Loose Ends*, p. 1.
26 Bernstein, "Helping Young Children to Cope," p. 274.
27 Bettelheim, *Uses of Enchantment*, p. 24.

48 / Law, Freedom, and Story

Let us now consider the actual use of storytelling as a technique in therapy. Interestingly enough, acknowledgement has been made of the long tradition of healing stories in religion. Carl Fellner and Robert Ornstein, for example, each point to the power of Sufi teaching narratives as "an ancient, yet irreplaceable, method of arranging and transmitting a knowledge that cannot be put in any other way."[28] Bettelheim cites the practice in traditional Hindu medicine of having disturbed individuals meditate on a fairy tale that gives form to their problems and suggests possible resolutions.[29]

One of the early works employing this technique in modern practice is Richard Gardner's *Therapeutic Communication with Children: The Mutual Storytelling Technique*. Gardner has his young patients pretend that they are on his TV program and invites them to tell a story to the audience, which is taped and played back for their amusement. He understands such stories as symbolic expressions of the child's situation and frequently offers classical psychoanalytic interpretations. (A forest fire stands for threatening emotions and a cave is the unconscious.) The therapist then answers with a story, adopting the basic format of the child's account, but modifying the plot to suggest a more creative response to the child's situation. There is nothing very subtle about the exchange of messages, as Gardner sees it. Children, feeling unloved by their parents and filled with terrifying anger, tell a story about a rabbit who is an "orphan" because his father is away in the navy and his mother is very sad. Gardner describes the same rabbit and the day when the rabbit realizes that his parents want to have more time with him because they really love him; in fact, they were spending more time but the little rabbit had not noticed. Moreover, the rabbit learns that he could get angry at times and nothing too terrible would happen; his parents would still love him. By exchanging these insights in story form, however, "the therapist speaks in the child's own language and thus has a good chance of 'being heard.' One could almost say that here the therapist's interpretations bypass the conscious and are received directly by the unconscious."[30] The lesson becomes more palatable in narrative form. Gardner twice quotes with approval from *The Yeoman of the Guard*: "in a merry guise, unpleasant truths are

28 Carl Fellner, "The Use of Teaching Stories in Conjoint Family Therapy," *Family Process* 15:4 (1976), p. 428. Robert Ornstein, *The Psychology of Consciousness* (New York: Penguin Books, 1975), passim.
29 Bettelheim, *Uses of Enchantment*, p. 25.
30 Richard A. Gardner, *Therapeutic Communication with Children: The Mutual Storytelling Technique* (New York: Science House, 1971), p. 18.

swallowed with a will—for he who'd make his fellow, fellow, fellow creatures wise should always gild the philosophic pill!"³¹ Again, little subtlety. The therapist always asks patients directly if they understand the moral of the stories, both the patients' and the therapist's. The former is regarded as diagnostic; the latter as prescriptive. The point is to alter the children's perception of their situation and suggest more creative responses. Progress occurs as the "therapist's messages gradually 'sink in' and become an intrinsic part of the child's personality structure."³² One recognizes this when patients begin to utilize the therapist's ideas in their own stories at both the conscious and the unconscious (i.e., symbolic) levels. Gardner frankly admits that this technique is akin to brainwashing, but argues that all therapy has this character. The most classical adult analyst who sits quietly listening "with only occasional catalytic comments . . . is imposing his own values on his patient."³³ Mutual storytelling is simply a more effective procedure with children.

The use of therapeutic storytelling has not been confined to the treatment of children. Robert Hobson, with a Jungian approach, suggests that a therapist may use "*cultural analogies . . . sometimes cast in the form of stories . . .* to supply *information which is new to the patient* but which is relevant to his present problem, within and without the therapeutic interview."³⁴ Similarly, Carl Fellner uses stories in conjoint family therapy because the successive layers of meaning in a tale carry "a message or comment on several levels not only of understanding but also of impact."³⁵ This avoids exclusively intellectual patterns of comprehension, allowing each member of the family group to make his or her own appropriation of the narrative. Moreover, the intricacies of a plot, both directly expressed and developed in the listener's mind, effectively signal the reality of "an interactional, circular, or oscillating chain of cause-effect-cause-etc." such as is operative in most situations.³⁶

In dealing with children, Gardner mentions the value of using "non-verbal communications, intonations, and humorous interjections, which are emotionally arousing to the child"³⁷ to increase the

31 Ibid., p. 281.
32 Ibid., p. 100.
33 Ibid., p. 102.
34 Robert F. Hobson, "Imagination and Amplification in Psychotherapy," *Journal of Analytical Psychology* 16:1 (1971), p. 98.
35 Fellner, "Use of Teaching Stories," p. 428.
36 Ibid., p. 429.
37 Gardner, *Therapeutic Communication with Children*, p. 231.

effectiveness of the story. In his *Therapeutic Metaphors* David Gordon has carried this further to develop a rich procedure for composing narratives that have proven to be effective in adult therapy. With any counseling, the first task is to gain some understanding of the clients' situation and how they wish to change it. Their goals, furthermore, must be "well-formed," that is, they must be clearly stated and entail matters over which the clients have some meaningful control. Unlike Gardner, Gordon does not invite his adult patients to provide his diagnostic insights by telling him stories. Rather he employs more traditional conversation, intended to elucidate the full reality, the "deep structure" behind the presented materials. (His thinking here, as elsewhere, is openly influenced by the work of Bandler and Grinder in *The Structure of Magic*.) Narrative enters the process in the treatment phase where Gordon composes fanciful stories (which he refers to as "metaphors") specifically for the particular patient. These metaphorical communications help the "client recover for himself a more complete, significant, and explicit representation of the experiences he is grappling with."[38] Besides giving insight, these tales provide vicarious experiences and become vehicles "for indirectly suggesting and/or implementing changes in patterns of coping."[39]

The stories are, of necessity, tailor-made to meet the client's needs as discovered in the diagnostic exchanges. Consequently, they must be isomorphic with the counselee's situation; the characters and events in the fiction must maintain an equivalent relationship to that in real life. Thus a man caught in conflict between his angry wife and his cold employer might be told a tale of the poor peasant having to endure a nagging wife while he works the land of the aloof baron. Even such simple parallelism can be effective in some cases, but Gordon goes on to develop much more richly the structure of his stories which, he believes, greatly enhances their therapeutic power. To begin with, he uses Virginia Satir's modes or styles of communication. Satir sets forth four basic patterns that tend to characterize styles of relating, or at least, behaviour under certain circumstances. These she calls "the placater," "the blamer," "the computer," and "the distracter." Each uses distinctive phrases and mannerisms. According to Gordon, careful observation suggests that not only do individuals have such characteristic styles but "most or all of the parts

---

38 David Gordon, *Therapeutic Metaphors* (Cupertino, Calif.: Meta Publications, 1978), p. 90.
39 Ibid., p. 54.

belonging to a person will have associated with it one of the Satir categories."[40] In telling his stories, Gordon employs language appropriate to the Satir posture of the various parties, be they representative of individuals or elements within a given person. The cold, computer boss becomes the insensitive recluse in the manor house and the blaming wife becomes the shrill, nagging shrew of the farmhouse. He further enhances the effect of the narrative by noting the representational systems involved. Bandler and Grinder have observed that most people encode experience primarily in terms of one of the senses; we tend to incorporate the world basically by kinesthetic, auditory, or visual inputs. This is quickly discernible by noting the patients' vocabulary. Visual individuals probably talk of seeing things clearly or of how things appear to them. Auditory individuals hear what another is saying, but is sure the latter was not listening to them. Kinesthetic people are shaken by the experience and know how another must feel. Gordon goes yet further to develop sub-modalities within these systems, distinguishing, for example, among texture, colour, and form within visual awareness. He incorporates his insights into representational systems and the sub-modalities at work in individuals into their fictional counterparts, thereby achieving fuller presentation of the dynamics of the real life drama.

Stories, however, must do more than reproduce the patients' situation. "What is significant about a therapeutic story is that *it preserves within it the relationships and coping patterns which operate in the 'real' problem, and that it provides a solution to the problem.*"[41] Gordon sometimes does this directly by having the characters gain freeing insights or develop new coping strategies. On other occasions he works more subtly, leading patients to new understanding by encouraging them to change their representational system or their Satir stance. In other words, the corresponding actor in the drama makes such shifts. Clearly, we have a process that is far more complex and sophisticated than that offered by Gardner, for the naive parallelism of Gardner's approach to children will not serve well with adults, especially those who—perhaps unconsciously—are seeking to thwart the therapeutic process.

> One of the most helpful side-effects of including in a metaphor Satir categories, representational systems, and/or sub-modality distinctions, is that these patterns of experience operate on a level that is so subtle that few, if any, clients are likely to be aware of (let alone

40 Ibid., p. 73.
41 Ibid., p. 20 (his emphasis).

comprehend) their occurrence or significance. What this means is that it can be irrelevant whether a metaphor is covert or not, provided that the changes effected on these subtler levels are themselves sufficient to effect the desired changes. . . . The fairy tale itself was merely a vehicle for making those experiential shifts.[42]

Again we may raise the question of manipulation. Gordon does employ strongly suggestive techniques in the middle of the story, even to including "imbedded commands" which are directed toward the client by name.[43] Yet he asserts that patients will only follow subtle advice such as truly fits their case. They are not totally malleable in the hands of the skilled storyteller.

At this point one might gain the impression that the sole impact of stories in psychotherapy is indirect, through the insinuation of quite distinct yet complex meanings. Stories illuminate by way of example. They clarify the patients' situation by means of fictional parallels, hinting of possible solutions. In this sense, they heal by expanding or building upon the patients' existing understanding of their situation. In terms of our last chapter, they are seen in mythic functioning.

Narrative, however, possesses another potential. It may in fact facilitate change by challenging, even disrupting, the patients' world-taken-for-granted; it may be parabolic. Jay Haley has drawn attention to the use of "therapeutic paradoxes" to force the counselee "to break free of his past ways of conceptualizing reality and meeting situations."[44] He cites, in this context, the koan in Zen. Individuals are presented with a situation that forces them to question their whole system for ordering experience. Carl Whitaker has made a similar point, referring to the method as the "psychotherapy of the absurd," where the goal is likened to Zen enlightenment experiences, achieved through reflection upon a koan. The therapist makes a "deliberate effort to break old patterns of thought and behavior."[45] "The use of deliberate obscurantism makes it necessary for the audience not only to *recognize* a body of thought but also to *learn* it. In contrast, direct presentation many times leads to recognition but results in a failure to learn."[46] Story can be a medium for precisely this effect. The primary impact of a narrative may not be to give a model

42 Ibid., pp. 158-59 (his emphasis).
43 Ibid., pp. 54-55.
44 Jay Haley, *Strategies of Psychotherapy* (New York: Grune & Stratton, 1963), p. 180.
45 Carl Whitaker, "Psychotherapy of the Absurd," *Family Process* 14:1 (1975), p. 11.
46 Ibid., p. 10 (his emphasis).

Story and Fantasy in Psychotherapy / 53

for behaviour, or to offer a path to success within the already accepted context, but rather to disrupt that whole vision which opens the way for radically new thinking. While therapists seem aware of the therapeutic potential of such disruption, not much attention has been paid to the use of stories directly for this purpose. This is not to imply that no recognition has been given. Fellner, for example, points out that stories can provide "a unique mixture of education and paradox,"[47] and alludes particularly to religious usage in the Sufi, Chasidic, and Zen traditions. (Therapists seem to regard the parables of Jesus as purely example stories. They may, of course, be forgiven since this has also been the dominent view among most Western religionists.)

> By telling a teaching story to a family, one has in some ways put them into a double-bind position. If the therapist says: "I will tell you a story," he clearly signals his intent to give them a message, yet the message that he gives is intentionally ambiguous and multidimensional.[48]

I suggest that this last remark points to yet another dimension of narrative expression that has healing significance and that has been recognized by counselors, namely, the openness of stories. By inviting our imaginative participation, the storyteller, while providing us with some picture of reality, some model, some world in which to live, is also inviting us to play in it, to modify or even reject it, for—after all—it is a story. So Bettelheim, referring to the importance of the fairy tale, stresses that its message may imply solutions but it never spells them out. "Fairy tales leave to the child's fantasizing whether and how to apply to himself what the story reveals about life and human nature."[49] Similarly, Gordon urges a deliberate vagueness in his therapeutic metaphors—despite their tailor-made character. One should not be too specific. "By intentionally refraining from specifying information, actions, and experiences of the characters within the metaphor, we free its audience to derive and employ their own interpretations of what is 'really going on.'"[50] Thus one utilizes "unspecified verbs" and "nouns lacking referential index." The net effect, as Gordon sees it, is to offer a picture of reality and some solution to the problem, yet in a way that is open to modification by the listeners. For their own purposes, the listeners may disrupt the

47 Fellner, "Use of Teaching Stories," p. 428.
48 Ibid.
49 Bettelheim, *Uses of Enchantment*, p. 45.
50 Gordon, *Therapeutic Metaphors*, p. 51.

story in the sense that the teller meant it. Consequently, such narrative can be more readily and personally appropriated. The combination of education and ambiguity, either as paradox (Fellner, Whitaker) or openness (Bettelheim, Gordon), means that it is "up to the individuals themselves to make their own discoveries, their own interpretation, and thus move toward possibly perceiving relationships in a new way, toward 'tasting' new realities."[51] Gordon makes a kindred point:

> The hope underlying this story-telling is that the experiences of another in overcoming a problem which is similar to that of the client's will suggest to him directly or indirectly ways in which he can deal with the situation. . . . If the story's resolution does not fit for him, he will at least know that a resolution is possible and perhaps begin searching for one (for many therapists, this is often the primary "reason" for relating such anecdotes.)[52]

Here one must acknowledge a distinct division among therapists. Gardner is very concerned that the patient recognize the moral of the story. Implicit in this approach is the assumption that the story has only one meaning, or at least a most important meaning known by the counselor. On the other hand, those wishing to foster the creative potential of openness in stories reject attempts to specify their meaning. Let stories remain stories! "One must never 'explain' to the child the meaning of fairy tales," Bettelheim argues, for "[s]uch simplifications and a directly stated moral turn this potential fairy tale into a cautionary tale which spells everything out completely. Thus the hearer's imagination cannot become active in giving the story a personal meaning."[53]

The Reappraisal of Fantasy

We have considered stories as they relate to the narrative sense of personal (and group) identity and as a dramatic means of gently conveying certain insights and suggestions, a means open to multiple levels of meaning in the message delivered and even a means to disrupting it. Both have relevance for psychotherapy, yet neither catches the full experience of storytelling for most people. Stories invite us to escape, to celebrate, to play, to dream.

Stories invoke the realm of the child and of fantasy, but it is not surprising that initially this went unrecognized, for Freud, as the

---

51 Fellner, "Use of Teaching Stories," p. 429.
52 Gordon, *Therapeutic Metaphors,* pp. 18-19.
53 Bettelheim, *Uses of Enchantment,* pp. 155, 168-69.

founder of the modern psychotherapeutic movement, essentially devalued fantasy as an infantile remnant. He was the champion of the rational and verbal, the so-called secondary process which, in the adult, must replace the non-rational and symbolic primary process. Bertha Mook suggests that this may simply reflect the times, that Freud's patients suffered from highly personalized, inner existences which no one, including the patients, could understand in terms of the shared meanings of the culture. Thus the task of therapy was the translation of this unconscious material into the rational and verbal. Today's patient, by contrast, "tends to be oversocialized but he does not know himself nor others anymore. He tends to hold on to conventional ways of behavior without personal participation."[54] The contemporary therapeutic task entails awakening for patients the whole depth of their personal experiences, and this leads to a new appraisal of fantasy. "Man first learns to know and understand his world through imagery."[55] Whether or not we fully accept this analysis, there is clearly a changing attitude in counseling circles concerning fantasy. Hillman, for instance, states that "fantasy is the dominant force in a life. One learns in therapy that fantasy is a creative activity which is continually telling a person into now this story, now that one."[56] Mook asserts that creativity is linked directly with the capacity to think in images. Thus the general experience of fantasizing, a deep part of the human experience of hearing and telling stories, now finds an opening in therapy. In much of its expression, fantasy as found in therapy has remained sheer fantasy in the widest sense of the imaginative, free play of the mind, although sometimes stories are used specifically with this intent.

Without assuming to reject Mook's analysis of the origins of this shift towards fantasy, let me cite three broad areas where changes in psychological thinking have played an important part in initiating these developments, namely, modifications in the view of the unconscious begun with Jung, the introduction of the concept of the bicameral mind and the new evaluation of the positive nature of the childlike in the adult.

What is the basic character of the material arising from the depths of the mind, from the unconscious, which appears so often in fanciful and symbolic forms? Freud cited at least two types. Some he

54 Bertha Mook, "Words and Images in Psychotherapy," *Psychotherapy: Theory Research and Practice* 12:2 (1975), pp. 212-13.
55 Ibid., p. 214.
56 Hillman, *Loose Ends*, p. 2.

recognized to be the memories of early childhood that had never been given verbal representation, coming from a time before the child had developed such thought systems. These live only in concrete and frequently distorted images. For example, the infant's experience of joy, fear, or frustration in relation to the mother would continue in such memories. Difficulties can exist in the present because there is no possibility of effective verbal recollection and reporting of this material. One can only hope to relive the experience, working it through more effectively. As is well known, however, Freud thought of the unconscious primarily as a mass of repressed material. The vast majority of images arising from it, such as in the fragmentary narratives and vignettes one experiences in dreams, were regarded as disguised expressions of these repressed ideas and emotions that were translated into the vocabulary of the primary process and thereby able to escape the vigilant eye of the censor.

With Jung one encounters a radically different conception. The repressed and largely negative dimensions of the individual are still there, constituting what Jung terms "the shadow," but this is only a small portion of a reality that has great potential as a creative factor. The unconscious is believed to fill a complementary relationship with the conscious mind. If individuals habitually devalue others, for instance, they are quite apt to dream of their victims in a very flattering way. In this vein, Fromm points out that depending upon the character of our conscious life, our dreams can reveal a higher as well as a lower self. "We are not only less reasonable and less decent in our dreams as Freud tended to assume but... we are also more intelligent, wiser, and capable of better judgment when we are asleep than when we are awake."[57] Jung speaks of the unconscious as having a "guiding function." "I realized that dreams were not just fantasies, but self-representations of unconscious developments which allowed the psyche of the patient gradually to grow out of the pointless personal tie."[58] In short, dreams have a goal in view. Indeed, the first dream that patients present in analysis often contains a symbolic representation of the problem together with a hint of the solution. In contrast to Freud, Jung assumes that the unconscious does not disguise material to deceive the conscious mind. Rather, speaking metaphorically, it wants to get its message across but in its own, highly symbolic, language.

57 Erich Fromm, *The Forgotten Language* (New York: Reinhart, 1951), p. 33.
58 C. G. Jung, "The Relations Between the Ego and the Unconscious," in *The Basic Writings of C. G. Jung* (New York: Modern Library, 1959), p. 115.

Story and Fantasy in Psychotherapy / 57

Among others, Ira Progoff has developed this view of the unconscious, seeing in it a way to understand the non-rational intuitions that are so often a part of creative breakthroughs. "The style by which the unconscious functions is thus primarily not repressive but purposive."[59] He insists that while Freud speaks of the contents of the unconscious as symbols, they are treated as signs in the sense that the dream contents stand for something else to which they point, and which could completely replace the dream images without loss. A true symbol, unlike this, is

> a spontaneous image which emerges from the depth of the personality and acts as a vehicle by which the potential latent in the unconscious of the individual can be carried forward. The symbol embodies the open future as that future is becoming present in the seed-depths of the individual.[60]

Consequently, the task of therapy, in relation to the unconscious, is less a matter of psychoanalysis than of psyche-evoking, "a rousing to activity of potentials that are inherent in the organic depths of the person, by which intimations of meaning are drawn forth out of the dark core of the psycho-physical unity of being."[61] One might, of course, question the degree of optimism contained in the growth assumptions inherent in such views of the unconscious. It is clear, in any case, that we have a radically different image of the mind, one conducive to a more positive interest in its symbolic materials as a source of insight and guidance.

Introducing a different perspective on the place of fantasy and symbolism in thought, contemporary research into the psychology of consciousness offers what could be seen as yet another and quite distinct image of what has been called the unconscious.[62] It presents us with a physiological basis for the existence of two complementary forms of consciousness. Uniquely, the human brain is composed of two hemispheres with quite distinct qualities. The right hemisphere correlates with the left side of the body and the left hemisphere with the right. But they operate in contrasting ways psychically, which is pertinent to this study. The left hemisphere is the primary seat of linear, analytical, and logical thinking, supporting our verbal and mathematical abilities. The right hemisphere relates to more holistic,

59   Ira Progoff, *The Symbolic and the Real* (New York: Julian Press, 1963), p. 71.
60   Ibid., p. 23.
61   Ibid., pp. 52-53.
62   Robert E. Ornstein, *The Psychology of Consciousness* (Harmondsworth: Penguin Books, 1975), passim.

relational, and patterned thought. It has limited skill in the area of language but makes possible our orientation in space, the recognition of shapes, including human faces, and much of our artistic aptitudes. Consequently, an injury to the right hemisphere may leave language functioning unaffected but cause severe disturbances in spatial awareness and musical ability; injury to the left hemisphere usually leaves the latter functions unimpaired, while disrupting language and mathematical skills. Finally, it appears that these two hemispheres relate to different aspects of the nervous system. "Verbal thoughts most directly affect the somatic [voluntary] nervous system. . . . [T]he other language, that of imagery, directly affects the autonomic nervous system (ANS), which regulates breathing, heartbeat, blood chemistry, . . . and many other bodily functions essential to life."[63] The swing of attention to fantasy, symbol, and imagery is a turn towards another dimension of consciousness, but one that is not available to us in verbal formulation, and that is, therefore, "unconscious" in Freud's sense. Yet clearly this is a form of consciousness that relates centrally to our total being and influences profoundly our psychological and physical functioning.

The psychology of consciousness reveals that our awareness can only capture a small portion of the mass of internal and external stimuli that impinges upon us, influencing and even potentially guiding our behaviour and thought in creative ways. Given our natural need to function in relation to the external environment—seeking food, avoiding dangers, etc.—"it would seem that we need to learn early in life to ignore the stream of 'internal' imagery much of the time."[64] The heavy emphasis upon rational and verbal skills in our Western educational systems has intensified this tendency to "hear" only the messages from the left hemisphere. In order to gain fuller life and greater balance mentally, we need "education in the intuitive mode" which, for Ornstein and others, means a serious engagement with the esoteric psychologies of the East and found in Buddhism, Sufism, and Yoga. But this is a massive adjustment for most of us. Ornstein comments:

> Since Western education is heavily dominated by the verbal-analytical mode, the procedure of the traditional esoteric

63 Dennis T. Jaffe and David E. Bresler, "The Use of Guided Imagery as an Adjunct to Medical Diagnosis and Treatment," *Journal of Humanistic Psychology* 20:4 (1980), p. 46.
64 Jerome L. Singer, "Theoretical Implications of Imagery and Fantasy Techniques," *Contemporary Psychoanalysis* 8:1 (1971), p. 84.

> psychologies may seem a bit strange at first. Their function, however, is to open up the other mode of knowledge, the complement of the normal one. They are primarily concerned with questions that are usually left out of or ignored with the Western tradition. . . . These exercises and techniques are, then, attempts to answer the questions left out of science and logical inquiry, attempts carried out intuitively and personally rather than in formal intellectual terms.[65]

We are called upon to turn away from the stimuli of the world and sit quietly, to slow the breathing and let the mind come to rest, to be deaf to the externals that we may hear at last our own inner depths. This entails "a shift away from the active, outward-oriented, linear mode toward the receptive and quiescent mode, and usually a shift from an external focus of attention to an internal one."[66] Much of this is familiar to those with any knowledge of meditation practices; much, too, finds its way into the various therapies involving mental imaging and inner fantasies.

Let me cite briefly one additional factor in the rise of fantasy as a serious factor in therapy, namely, the re-evaluation of the childlike. We have already noted the tie between symbolic language and fantasy and the preverbal experiences of childhood. Naturally, on a more immediate and everyday level of thought, we tend to associate fantasy with children. The new note in therapy is the call, not to dismiss such aspects of personality as childish, but to affirm the childlike dimensions in the adult.

> Fantasy in our view is the attempt of the psyche to re-mythologize consciousness. . . . Soul-making goes hand in hand with deliteralizing consciousness and restoring its connection to mythic and metaphorical thought patterns. . . . Literalism is sickness. . . . Story is prophylactic. . . . So the first task, as I see it, is restorying the adult.[67]

Most specifically transactional analysis uses this conceptualization. It talks of three basic ego states: the Parent, the Adult, and the Child. The Child is that part of us that feels and thinks as we did when we were children. It is where our emotions find most natural expression. While it is by no means advisable for the mature individual to function as a child, transactional analysis places great emphasis on the importance of keeping in touch with the Child in us, meaning the playful, emotional, and fantasizing aspects of the self. "The value of the Child should not be underestimated. It is said to be the best part of a person

65 Ornstein, *Psychology of Consciousness*, pp. 163-64.
66 Ibid., p. 123.
67 Hillman, *Loose Ends*, pp. 3-4.

and the only part that can really enjoy itself. It is the source of spontaneity, sexuality, creative change, and is the mainspring of joy."[68]

Fantasy and Therapy

Given the free flowing form of fantasy, not surprisingly it expresses itself in a variety of forms in therapy. Some specific styles will emerge in our examination of its applications in counseling. It might be helpful, however, just to sketch some broad general patterns appearing in treatment.

H. Leuner developed a technique which he called "guided affective imagery."[69] Patients lie down on a couch or relax in a chair and close their eyes. A mildly hypnoid state usually develops, following which the patients are invited to imagine themselves in a series of ten standard settings. They describe the scene and what is happening. These tableaux include being in a meadow, climbing a mountain, following a stream, discovering a cave, etc. Leuner believed that each was a different universal symbol. The meadow was a fairly neutral return to nature, the mountain climb a struggle for higher goals, the cave an encounter with one's own threatening depths. If the patients run into difficulties, the therapist suggests ways to imagine overcoming them. The patients, blocked from reaching the mountain top, might be told to descend part way and look for another path. The whole experience continues on this essentially symbolic and narrative level.

Ira Progoff devised "twilight imaging." Here again the clients relax, opening themselves to symbolic consciousness, but the therapist offers no suggestions to initiate reflection. Rather, the patient "permits himself to observe and describe the flow of imagery that moves upon the screen of his mind's eye."[70]

> The primary quality of Twilight Imagery lies not in its visualness, but in its *twilightness*, the fact that it takes place, as though by itself, on the intermediary, or twilight, level of consciousness. The term *imagery* refers to the fact that its main expressions are not literal in the sense of being thoughts or ideas, but that they are rather representational or symbolic. They may indeed be visual, as they often are; but in many cases they are not visual at all. They may take the form of

68 Steiner, *Scripts People Live*, p. 29.
69 H. Leuner, "Guided Affective Imagery: A Method of Intensive Psychotherapy," *Journal of Psychotherapy* 23 (1969), pp. 4-23.
70 Progoff, *The Symbolic and the Real*, p. 92.

perceptions that come through any of the other, non-visual senses. But they are *inward* perceptions.[71]

Only after recording the stream of images is the person able to reflect upon their meaning. The therapist makes no input into the process, other than inviting the patient to engage in it.

Frederick Perls, the founder of gestalt psychology, also uses fantasy. He invites people, either in group settings or alone, to look carefully at their dreams and then play the various roles depicted, including those of inanimate objects. For instance, a patient describes a dream wherein she sees a lake drying up and a circle of porpoise-like creatures stumbling about, waiting to die.[72] As the water recedes she thinks that she will at least find some treasure on the bottom but discovers only an old license plate. Perls invites her to play the part of the license plate, describing how she feels, how she got there, etc. Later she plays the part of the lake. One notes here some direction by the therapist in suggesting which parts of the dream to adopt.

To return to Progoff's work, he uses a verbal—as well as a visual—type of fantasy. Clients are asked to engage in conversation with other people, living or dead, with events in their past, or even with parts of their own bodies. They literally write out an imaginary dialogue. (I said . . . or mother said . . . or my lungs said . . . .)

Of what value are such fantasy techniques in therapy? Images and symbols, especially in the form of dreams, have long been regarded as omens in many cultures, but in therapy they become diagnostic signs, "the royal road to the unconscious," as Freud put it. Through the interpretation of dreams, the deciphering of their symbolism, Freud discerned the nature of neurosis. Jung had a kindred interest in dreams, although (as we have seen) he considered them a direct attempt by the unconscious to illuminate the client's distress. Likewise, various fantasy techniques can serve a diagnostic function. Paul Kosbab specifically makes this point regarding the patient's responses to Leuner's ten standard scenes in his guided affective imagery.

> All these elements are, of course, the patient's own projections and as such diagnostically important. While some may immediately see a pleasant green meadow, bathed in warm sunshine, and reflecting a general feeling of emotional and psychological well-being, other patients may visualize nothing but bare soil, with perhaps a few

---

71 Progoff, *At a Journal Workshop*, p. 78 (his emphasis).
72 Frederick S. Perls, *Gestalt Therapy Verbatim* (Lafayette, Calif.: Real People Press, 1969), pp. 81-82.

> patches of dried-out grass; or a barren desert—indicating a state of impoverished emotional life or depression.[73]

Ira Progoff urges that twilight imaging be recorded in the patients' journals in order to help them gradually develop a fuller awareness of the depths of their own situation. Similar techniques have been employed by a number of therapists in the treatment of physical disease patterns. Theirs is the belief that "somatic" illness inevitably has spiritual, psychological, and social elements in its etiology (Booth, Simon, Jaffe, etc.). In some instances, new patients are asked to image spontaneous pictures of their present condition.

> These pictures can lead to important information not only about illnesses but also about the patients' beliefs, hopes, expectations, and fears about their bodies, the body's ability to withstand the illness, and the effectiveness of the recommended treatment. Many patients have uncannily accurate intuitions about their illnesses, and the imagery process can make these available to the diagnostician to add to the other sources of information.[74]

Such symbolization also allows for psychological interpretations of the meaning of symptoms in ways not otherwise accessible. Carl and Stephanie Simonton suggest, in addition, that such symbols often make fairly accurate assessments of the prognosis.[75] The images are part of a self-fulfilling prophecy and, needless to say, have implications for therapeutic interventions.

What then of fantasy as a therapeutic device, in contrast to a diagnostic one? Although the most dramatic and powerful effects are achieved through the active use of fantasy, together with the help of a counselor, nonetheless, significant results have been reported in cases where patients simply let the imagery flow through the mind. "If nothing else is done than continuous imagery . . . there is an enormous release of tension, an intense catharsis, accompanied by emotional outbursts which often assume vehement forms."[76] Obvious parallels exist here with the early abreaction therapy, practised by Freud and Breuer, in which patients found symptomatic relief through re-experiencing past traumas, thereby allowing a fuller emotional reaction to them.

73 Paul Kosbab, "Imagery Techniques in Psychiatry," *Archives of General Psychiatry* 31 (1974), p. 285.
74 Jaffe and Bresler, "Use of Guided Imagery," p. 49.
75 Simonton, *Getting Well Again*, pp. 140-42.
76 Augusta Jellinek, "Spontaneous Imagery," *American Journal of Psychotherapy* 3 (1949), p. 382.

Story and Fantasy in Psychotherapy / 63

Fantasy, or at least the use of the imagination, has also been employed in some forms of behaviour modification therapy. Images are viewed as surrogate stimuli or responses with quite limited and specific meaning. They are treated as signs rather than symbols. (Behaviour therapists tend to ignore their rather fluid and rich complexity.) In treating phobias, for instance, adult patients may be encouraged to imagine themselves in increasingly fear-producing situations and then be helped to practise relaxation techniques to quiet their anxiety. Children, harder to train in these relaxation skills, are encouraged to imagine fear-producing situations but to turn them into enjoyable fantasies. In one case, a child's fear of visiting the dentist was treated by having him imagine himself on various adventures with Batman and Robin. Later, he accompanied them to the dentist where they had their teeth fixed, and then he imagined himself in the chair with his friends watching him. He was finally able to visit the dentist with little fear.[77] Of greater interest to our present purposes than either the purely abreactive or behaviour modification approaches, however, is the therapy that allows an even fuller participation in fantasy.

Fantasy is used with somatic disorders in the form of imaging a preferred condition. For example, "a woman seeking relief from bronchial pain experienced reduced suffering and had her lungs clear considerably following a procedure of imaging the clogged passages draining."[78] The Simontons report significant benefit with patients who are taught to relax and then to image the diseased portion of the body functioning properly.[79] In another context, athletes have found that by relaxing in a chair and imaging themselves successfully accomplishing various acts, they actually improve their performance level.[80]

For the most part, therapists employing fantasy have tended to utilize active, dramatic means, some of which assuredly sound bizarre to our rational and disciplined thinking. The Gouldings, strongly influenced by transactional analysis, employ redecision therapy, invoking the Free Child, often coupled with actual memories. "In redecision therapy the client experiences the child part of self, enjoys his childlike qualities, and creates fantasy scenes in which he can

77 Anees Sheikh and Nancy Panagiotou, "Use of Mental Imagery in Psychotherapy," *Perceptual and Motor Skills* 41 (1975), p. 562.
78 Dennis Jaffe, *Healing From Within* (New York: Alfred A. Knopf, 1980), p. 249.
79 Simonton, *Getting Well Again*, pp. 125-39.
80 Jaffe, *Healing From Within*, pp. 233-34.

safely give up the constricting decisions he made in childhood....
[T]his time he *does the scene the way he wants to do it.*"[81] A man
frightened by the dark since childhood visualizes himself as a child at
home alone at night and dramatically encounters his fear. He imagines ugly goblins and chases them away, perhaps to the cheers of
others in the group. To be sure, not all scenes involve childhood
memories. Some are pure fantasy. A woman visualizes herself
paddling a tiny canoe through her arteries and veins till she comes on
the source of her pain, which she subsequently images and sees
going away.[82] Jaffe and the Simontons have effectively used such
procedures on physical disease, pain, and "psychological" realities
such as resentment and fear of death. The Simontons work particularly with cancer patients, coupling meditation and mental imagery
with traditional medical treatment. Patients visualize their radiation or
chemotherapy attacking the cancerous cells, and especially their
body's own immune system rushing white blood cells to devour the
malignant intruders. They also "see" the tumour growing smaller.
Usually they are encouraged to draw pictures of their mental images.
This technique is therapeutic and tends to give a fair representation of
the prognosis as well. The doctors report, for example, a patient
named John who had several recurrences of his disease. He built his
images around the white blood cells,

> visualizing them as a vast army of white knights on white horses who
> would line up, their lances gleaming in the sunlight, and charge
> through the landscape killing cancer cells, which were small and
> slow-moving creatures.
>   But just prior to his two recurrences, John found his imagery
> changing. Sometimes he visualized black knights in the ranks of his
> army, which he took to mean enemy knights. At other times he
> imagined his knights' lances bent and limp, as if made of rubber, so
> that clearly they could do no damage.[83]

Now the question arises whether images are a cause or an effect
of the disease process. Or can they be both? Probably the somatic
examples of "successful" fantasies are the most astonishing to the
average reader.

A last variant in technique involves what one could call engaging
the self's inner wisdom in fantasy conversation, as in Progoff's intensive journal approach. The primary goal is to acquire insight into

81 Mary and Robert Goulding, *Changing Lives*, p. 9 (their emphasis).
82 Ibid., pp. 194-95.
83 Simonton, *Getting Well Again*, p. 142.

one's situation. Thus, in addition to developing a picture of pain and watching it grow smaller, patients may imagine the pain as some sort of creature and converse with it. They can inquire about why it is there, what message it brings, and what one must do for it to go away. Such conversations provide especially valuable instruction because it is derived from the patients themselves. Sometimes patients image an "inner guide"[84] or "inner advisor,"[85] possibly as a wise, older person, an elf, or even an animal to whom they may turn for direction.

> By creating and interacting with an inner advisor, a person learns to gather important information from their subconscious, and is able to feel comfortable and familiar with parts of themselves that had previously been inaccessible to conscious awareness.[86]

What do we make of all this? Is it not perchance escapist, living in the delusions of a dream world rather than facing reality? But surely as Perls phrases it, it makes sense to "withdraw to a situation from which you get support, and then come back with regained strength to reality."[87] Yet more can be said. "Mental imagery is not a method of self-deception; it is a method of self-direction."[88] Fantasy is a way to shape the psychological and physical course of the individual. In some cases the shaping is done by the therapist, even outside the comprehension of the patient. The latter may not be aware of the real meaning of the fantasy and, hence, will not impede the process through the actions of the censor. The therapist can then suggest possible solutions, again symbolically. It seems generally agreed, however, that therapy proves most effective when patients take charge of their own fantasies and invent their own dramatic solutions. "The less the therapist guides the patient, i.e., the fewer suggestions he gives and the less active he is, the better the therapy."[89]

While the whole process is narrative only in the sense of fantasy, drama, and the free imagination, nonetheless, this is an essential portion of such experience and very germane to our discussion. By and large, the techniques that focus on mental imagery and free fantasy have not used set stories, but one can still speculate that the

---

84 Ibid., p. 204.
85 Jaffe and Bresler, "Use of Guided Imagery," p. 54.
86 Ibid.
87 Perls, *Gestalt Therapy Verbatim*, p. 63.
88 Simonton, *Getting Well Again*, p. 139.
89 Max Hammer, "The Directed Daydream Technique," *Psychotherapy: Theory, Research and Practice* 4:4 (1967), p. 177.

power of narrative involves its capacity to relate to this fantasy dimension of the self. Moreover, Ornstein makes explicit reference to the use of tales precisely for this reason: "It is not, then, necessary to 'understand' the stories in the usual intellectual and rational mode."[90] One can recall here Gordon's appeal to the subtleties of his "metaphors" which slip past our normal levels of awareness.

The main feature to be stressed in all these therapies is their deep commitment to the power of fantasy. Regarding Jung's practice of the subjective amplification of dreams, Hobson contends, "The aim is not to trace fantasy to its origins in the past, but to facilitate an on-going creative process."[91] Similarly, Jellinek avows: "We do not try to dissolve or thoroughly interpret the symbols. They are brought to the subject's attention and he is told to use them consciously and purposefully in order to influence his own attitudes."[92] (Progoff actually notes that when clients become self-conscious and analytical about their fantasies, the latter lose their power. Psychoanalysis kills psyche-evoking.[93]) Sheikh and Panagiotou include such therapies among those that "have placed 'the healing of the psyche' back into the 'magical' model which emphasizes a transformation through irrational procedures as opposed to rational and reflex therapies."[94] One confronts the irrational source of anxiety, phobias, or pessimism on its own ground by employing irrational remedies. Even when dealing with highly sophisticated patients, "magical" therapies may be indicated. Jellinek reports treating a stutter in a twenty-four-year-old Ph.D. student in atomic physics with fantasy techniques. The patient found it hard to slow down his speech for fear that "[i]t will catch up with me." He was asked to visualize "it" and eventually saw a dwarf sitting on his shoulder. At this point the therapist suggested that if he talked slowly, the demon would starve to death. "This extremely intelligent boy understood very well that here he did not deal with rational processes, but with another psychic category."[95] We may again recall Hillman's words that literalism is the enemy; it is fantasy that is creative. Beyond all doubt, many people in our culture need help even to begin to recover this dimension of their lives.

We know that we live in our stories. We understand ourselves through complex narratives composed of actual or imagined

90 Ornstein, *Psychology of Consciousness*, p. 189.
91 Hobson, "Imagination and Amplification," p. 92.
92 Jellinek, "Spontaneous Imagery," p. 375.
93 Progoff, *The Symbolic and the Real*, p. 122.
94 Sheikh and Panagiotou, "Use of Mental Imagery," p. 557.
95 Jellinek, "Spontaneous Imagery," p. 380.

Story and Fantasy in Psychotherapy / 67

memories from our personal past or from the history of our communities. We relate to myths, legends, and ordinary fictions, setting forth our heroes and our dreams. Through story we keep telling ourselves who we are, what we must do, what we may hope for, where we are going. Such messages do more than set expectations and direct voluntary conduct. They significantly determine the future. They are self-fulfilling prophecies even when we are not fully conscious of them. The woman who continually reminds herself that she cannot expect to succeed because she is a loser will likely prove to be a loser. The macho male who holds, even unconsciously, the hero image of the "tough guy" will continue to be threatened by any intimations of his own tenderness and thus be restricted in this facet of his functioning. The same is true even at the purely somatic level.

> The utility of a therapeutic approach to the use of mental imagery in health care is evident when one notices that patients are always using imagery to send messages to their bodies. These images can significantly affect the patient's progress in therapy, for in many cases, the images transmitted are highly negative ones that inhibit the healing process. . . . When the imagination is preoccupied by these negative pictures, the autonomic nervous system is being told, in effect, "Prepare the body to be helpless. Don't even bother mobilizing the immune and inflammatory defences." . . . [T]hese messages become a self-fulfilling prophecy.[96]

In other words, we are highly suggestible, especially to repeated subconscious (thus uncriticized) messages, not to mention the self-images and hopes that they produce. Even when operating on a largely conscious level, their effects can be dramatic. The use of fantasy in therapy, it would seem, produces a means of rewriting our internal dramas, changing our images of the future and the self-imposed demands of the present, thus initiating a creative message to and about the self. Fantasy seems uniquely suitable because as a consciously chosen device it provides a link between the two types of consciousness (or between the conscious and the unconscious), drawing upon the wisdom of each and bringing their two understandings into harmony.

Yet perhaps there is more to fantasy than merely this power to correct and revive our personal stories, our inner messages of hope or despair. I suggest that we need to recognize the force and value of the fanciful moment in itself. *Fantasy is the mind at play*, and Winnicott argues that play is the arena of creativity.

96 Jaffe and Bresler, "Use of Guided Imagery," p. 47.

> The general principle seems to me to be valid that *psychotherapy is done in the overlap of the two play areas, that of the patient and that of the therapist.* If the therapist cannot play, then he is not suitable for the work. If the patient cannot play, then something needs to be done to enable the patient to become able to play, after which psychotherapy may begin. The reason why playing is essential is that it is in playing that the patient is being creative.[97]

It may be necessary to help the patient to evolve some terms of reference, some defining structures, some sense of identity, before he will be free to play. Fantasy as play will then liberate this creative force precisely because it grants us freedom from the structures, the order, the limitations of our inner dramas that are set by society or self-imposed. We need, in Winnicott's phrase, a new experience more than the right explanation, an experience of "a non-purposive state,"[98] that which Jaffe refers to as "passive volition,"[99] a freedom just to be. Any therapist who would encourage this playful creativity must, of necessity, be playful and must resist the temptation to stifle it through his own ordering interpretations.

> My description amounts to a plea to every therapist to allow for the patient's creativity to play, that is, to be creative in analytic work. The patient's creativity can be only too easily stolen by a therapist who knows too much. It does not really matter, of course, how much the therapist knows provided he can hide this knowledge, or refrain from advertising what he knows.[100]

There is a point at which the fantasy gives life and the interpretation kills.

In summary, therapeutic experience suggests at least three major elements in the dynamic power of storytelling. First, in its many forms, counseling supports Stephen Crites's contention concerning the narrative character of human experience.[101] We understand ourselves and our world largely in terms of a collection of tales and significant events, perhaps collapsed into symbols, drawn from our personal history and cultural traditions. These tales and events become welded into a personal story within which we live. Narrative would thus appear to be a form immediately relevant to influencing

97   D. W. Winnicott, *Playing and Reality* (London: Tavistock Publications, 1971), p. 54.
98   Ibid., p. 55.
99   Jaffe, *Healing From Within*, p. 197.
100   Winnicott, *Playing and Reality*, p. 57.
101   Stephen Crites, "The Narrative Quality of Experience," *Journal of the American Academy of Religion* 39 (1971), pp. 291-311.

basic human understandings, for it is the style in which, to a significant degree, they are already encoded. Second, we find support for the claim that stories are mythoparabolic. Evidence was found for the power of story to convey complex and dynamic interpretations of life. The diagnostic use of patients' fantasies and the didactic application of traditional and tailor-made stories by therapists both involve such a mythic function. We have also observed the use of story as a disruptive agency in therapy, therapeutic paradoxes, and the absurd, although this use has been given less emphasis. The Zen koan was explicitly cited in this regard. Third, we saw an increasing interest in the creative power of fantasy, especially when allowed simply to flow as uninterpreted flights of imagination and play. This underlines the need to recognize the important encoding of reality that takes place not in a rational and discursive logic, but through symbol and myth. It tells us, too, that healing comes with the surrender to a wisdom that is beyond our conceptual powers, with the opening of the self to experience rather than to mastery. This may indeed be part of that which religion speaks of as "faith" and "grace."

4
Structure and Anti-Structure in Social Processes

Turning now to the study of communities in sociology and anthropology, I shall not undertake as broad a survey as I did with story in psychotherapy. I wish to concentrate instead upon the writings of one man, Victor Turner. Turner's work is not, in the first instance, focused upon narrative in social process, yet his insights remain relevant for us. To begin with, it is argued by Turner and others that social processes in general have a narrative character. Societies and cultures must be seen as human rather than as natural products. We need, in Turner's phrase, to invoke the "humanistic coefficient"[1] in our theories, thus allowing for the dramatic qualities of choice, volition, purpose, and decision as crucial social determinants. Thus, for example, he speaks of "social dramas."[2] R. Harré and P. F. Secord make a similar point when they call for a "dramaturgical standpoint" from which to interpret social behaviour.[3] James Peacock urges the adoption of a "dramatistic" view of society:

1 Victor Turner, *Dramas, Fields, and Metaphors* (Ithaca: Cornell University Press, 1974), p. 33.
2 Ibid., passim.
3 R. Harré and P. F. Secord, *The Explanation of Social Behaviour* (Oxford: Basil Blackwell, 1972), pp. 205-26.

> Why not cast narrative in the starring role? Heed the power of narrative to structure and distill patterns underlying all phases of social process. View entire social processes as structured around and distilled by narrative form. In short: treat society as a narrative.[4]

Consequently, while Turner's studies focus upon social processes in broad perspective, it is not a violation of his interpretations to apply them to narrative experience per se. Moreover, in his works, he draws heavily upon the analysis of ritual which, in many ways, is itself enacted story and thus becomes a medium for participation in narrative experience. A major interpretive category, "liminality," for example, is derived from this study.

Emerging in the previous chapters as a major element in the dynamics of narrative experience was the interaction between the mythic and the parabolic, between the didactic and the disruptive function of stories, or, more broadly, between the affirming, ordering elements and the rejecting, disordering ones. I have maintained that the power of story to do both at once, to be mythoparabolic, makes it a peculiarly effective force. Turner helps us grasp such dynamics as they occur in societal processes, in the interaction between social structure and anti-structure. The latter appears both as pure anti-structure and as counter-structure, akin to Crossan's recognition of the parabolic and the counter-mythic. Of special interest is Turner's emphasis upon the positive potential within anti-structure. In contrast to the emphasis in Berger's *The Sacred Canopy*, leaving the security of structure, for Turner, offers rewards as well as risks. This chapter, then, will concentrate upon the dialectic of structure and anti-structure in society, and on the creative possibilities of anti-structure, seeking—by extension—to apply these to narrative. With Turner's interest in ritual, we shall find many examples of enacted story. Once more narrative proves to be mythoparabolic.

Structure in Social Process

Corresponding to the mythic in narrative or to identity in psychology (to the ordering principle) is the concept of social structure in anthropology and sociology. Here one thinks of the ordinary constellation of institutions and social roles, usually set within some hierarchical structure, that define functions, prerogatives, and duties for each element of the community. Using terms borrowed from

---

4 James L. Peacock, "Society as Narrative," in Robert F. Spencer (ed.), *Forms of Symbolic Action* (Seattle: University of Washington Press, 1969), p. 172.

Robert Merton, Turner refers to "'the pattern of role-sets, status-sets, and status-sequences' *consciously* recognized and regularly operative in a given society."[5] Society defines for us what it means to be a father, mother, citizen, college student, or president. We live with a similarly accepted ordering and definition of social institutions. The financial rewards to incumbents, the permissible forms of power exercised, the limits of acceptable patterns of behaviour, for everything from formalizing the relationship between the sexes to the design of government, all form part of our social structure. Paradoxically, Turner is at pains to stress that society is dynamic, that it is constantly changing and evolving. Consequently, the structures of which we speak are always in flux; the family, government, economic order, etc., are not fixed. Nevertheless, he argues that a structuring dynamism is shaping the way people understand and respond to the world. Of necessity, we organize and order our world; in Berger's terms we "nomize" reality. Turner writes:

> These individual and group structures, carried in people's heads and nervous systems, have a steering function, a "cybernetic" function, in the endless succession of social events, imposing on them the degree of order they possess, and, indeed, dividing processual units into phases.[6]

We are, in fact, investigating not a stable reality out there called the social structure, but rather the relatively stable patterns we use to interpret reality. Again we are dealing with a human ordering of experience. Our task is to examine from a sociological standpoint the processes involved in sustaining and transmitting these interpretive structures.

How is social structure maintained? In *The Sacred Canopy*, Peter Berger reminds us that social structure is most effectively supported (a nomos most secure) when it is simply taken for granted. Husbands who remain loyal to their wives and support their children, who dismiss all temptation to run off with other women because it would be literally unthinkable, by their loyal fulfillment of the nomos reaffirm and strengthen the social power of marriage. Berger refers to this as primary legitimation; it constitutes the source of the stability and security that comes with the automatic and uncritical acceptance of society's definitions. (Subsequently, we shall see that there is a very different, but in many ways equally powerful, means of legitima-

---

5 Turner, *Dramas, Fields, and Metaphors*, p. 237 (his emphasis).
6 Ibid., p. 36.

tion, one not discussed by Berger, the operation of socially sanctioned occasions for rebelling against the norm, times when one is given permission to transgress. Anti-structural or anti-nomic behaviour is in that case neutralized by being domesticated.)

For most cultures, death represents a powerful anomic threat, the spectre of a chaotic breakdown in shared hopes and values. Virtually all peoples, then, have organized socially recognized instruments for reaffirming, if indeed not re-establishing, the order, stability, and security of their communal existence in the face of death. Theodicies are the expression of this as purely intellectual systems. At a ritual level, funerals stand as socially evolved patterns, carried out for the purpose of sustaining a people against the anomic assault of death. Through dramatic actions, the community at large and the bereaved individual attest to the "eternal" character of the social order. These actions may appear meaningless or bizarre to outsiders, but within the culture they are rational and purposive. Among the Kotas of India, for instance, the mourning process continues for a period that may last up to a year or more. It begins with the "green funeral" at the time of death and ends with the "dry funeral" held every one or two years to mark the close of mourning for all deaths since the last such rite.[7] During the interval, a recent widow who has no son seeks to bear a child from another man, and any child conceived before the dry funeral is considered the offspring of the dead spouse. All this is intended to secure the continuance of the husband's line, to overcome the threat to orderly succession that death represents. Another custom, which at first appears odd, is that a widow or widower upon returning home from the dry funeral immediately has sexual relations with a sibling of the deceased. Yet within the nomos of the Kotas, the custom stands as an affirmation that living will continue in spite of death. Within our own Western culture one can recall the burial of the British monarchs: the slow dirge as the military brings the body on a gun carriage for interment at Windsor Castle, followed after the service by the same troops marching away to a rousing melody. Again the symbolism is clear. Society's order remains; life will go on; the nomos is not shattered. One can recall more recently the assassination of Lord Mountbatten. From the point of view of the IRA, this was an attack on the social order, a dramatic rejection of the British nomos expressed in Ulster. From the British perspective, the funeral, carried out with great

---

7 David G. Mandelbaum, "Social Uses of Funeral Rites," in Herman Feifel (ed.), *The Meaning of Death* (New York: McGraw-Hill, 1959), pp. 190-98.

drama and pomp, was a reassertion of the unshaken character of the British story, of the majesty, glory, and history of England, a ritual proclamation that despite this traumatic episode, the British social order remains unbroken. Obviously, similar factors were at work in the funeral for President Sadat where the presence of many heads of state was itself an affirmation of a global order.

Not only in the face of death do societies develop vehicles to sustain their shared meanings, but they also make wide use of specific, scholarly argumentation and dramatic, public ceremonials in order to keep alive the social structure generally. In *Symbol and Conquest*, Ronald Grimes offers a detailed analysis of the social rituals that are an important part of the cultural life of Santa Fe, New Mexico. These are particularly interesting for our present purposes since Grimes's work highlights some parallels and differences between these rituals and those detailed by Victor Turner that will assist us in clarifying the distinction between ritual as social affirmation and as social disruption.

Grimes points out that there are actually several levels or foci of social structure represented in Santa Fe, each with its own communal celebrations. The people of that city sense themselves to be members of several significant communities that order their lives around different, at times even conflicting, values and shared stories. For our purposes I need deal only with two of the major social rituals and with these merely in sufficient detail to bring out the matters of interest to our study.

A major cultural figure and symbol in the history of New Mexico is La Conquistadora, a representation of the Virgin Mary associated in history with the Spanish "reconquest" of New Mexico by Don Diego De Vargas in 1692. This supposedly bloodless re-establishment of Spanish culture and Catholic religion was, according to tradition, associated with the special intervention and power of the Virgin. In fact, La Conquistadora is an approximately three-foot-tall figure of Mary. Her full name reveals her civic as well as religious significance. She is Our Lady of the Rosary, the Conqueress, Queen, and Patroness of the Ancient Kingdom of New Mexico and the Royal City of Santa Fe.[8] Clearly, La Conquistadora stands, at the first level, as part of the Catholic ecclesial reality, but obviously she has taken on symbolic meanings also in relationship both to Hispanic ethnicity and to the civic sense of Santa Fe in general. Thus both Catholic Pueblo

---

8 Ronald L. Grimes, *Symbol and Conquest* (Ithaca: Cornell University Press, 1976), p. 219.

people and non-Catholic Anglos take part in some of the social ceremonies associated with her festivals. Unlike pilgrimages that Turner has studied in detail and to which we shall return, Grimes observes that the processions associated with this Santa Fe ritual involve no distancing of oneself from the social structure, but rather a dramatic celebration and assertion of the social structure. He remarks:

> The nonliminal, status system ethos of La Conquistadora and her processions is strong. The statue's home is the seat of the archbishop; she is at the heart of ecclesial power and order. And in her processions a definite hierarchical order maintains. Though some of the civil authorities who participate insist that they do so as devout individuals, not as community officials, the average participant still views them in terms of their statuses.[9]

Obviously both ecclesial and civic authority are represented. Unlike Our Lady of Guadalupe, La Conquistadora narrative makes no reference to any miraculous appearance of the Virgin. Indeed, "virtually no miracle tradition is associated with her."[10] She is very much part of the nomos of everyday life. The whole public celebration in early summer revolving around her is fundamentally a dramatic and powerful reassertion of some basic elements of Catholic faith, Hispanic culture, and, to some degree, civic pride. Such occasions are professions of faith, sacred displays of the symbols of one's allegiance, and thus restatements of commitment to the social order. In contrast to a Corpus Christi procession, here we see affirmed not only religious but also ethnic and civic meanings.

Late in the summer a second festival with an accompanying series of public rituals takes place. The primary focus is secular; it is a celebration more of civic and ethnic values than of religious ones, though again the symbols have multiple references. It is the same story, the reconquest, but now the focus is upon De Vargas, the military and political figure, and the message is harmony for all peoples of Santa Fe, especially Spanish and Pueblo, under the umbrella of Hispanic culture. The central ceremony here is the Entrada; in the style of medieval Spanish morality plays, it is a re-enactment of De Vargas's entrance into the city following an Indian uprising that had driven out the whites. Staged in the open air, the pageant involves the audience, deepening its impact and quickening the viewers' allegiance to the social values it affirms. It is truly a

---

9 Ibid., p. 68.
10 Ibid.

mass-involving social drama. The actual historic events involve De Vargas's coming to Santa Fe in 1692, his pleading with the Indians to surrender and to return to Spanish culture and the Catholic faith. After their initial rejection of this plea, De Vargas is said to have laid aside his arms and to have entered the city, accompanied only by La Conquistadora, whereupon the Pueblos immediately submitted without bloodshed. Thus harmony was re-established between the two groups. The story omits mentioning that De Vargas returned in 1693 with a larger force, demanding total surrender. When this was rejected, a battle broke out in which a number of Pueblos were killed and those who surrendered were given to De Vargas's troops as indentured labourers for ten years. The Entrada, portrayed in the modern pageant, begins with a conversation between two Pueblo leaders in the uprising. The speeches argue that "the revolt was not the result of racial hatred between Hispanos and Indians but was an aberration to be blamed on a few malcontent Indians and a few 'lousy, greedy' Spanish governors. Pope the revolutionary is made to refer to the Franciscans as 'those new amigos [who] were even poorer than we were.'"[11] Beyond all doubt, history has been rewritten in an attempt to assert that, despite the conflict, a fundamental racial harmony prevails. Later versions of the Entrada modify the language so that "apostasy" and "butchery" become "repudiation of faith" and "killing." This glosses over the intensity of the racial conflict.

> The pageant obviously focuses on 1692 alone in order to emphasize the historical grounds for harmonious Hispano-Indian relations. In fact, the moral of the pageant is that the contemporary "tricultural existence" is a direct result of De Vargas' peaceful and imaginative tactics. The pageant implies that De Vargas knew exactly what his deeds promised for future generations.[12]

Here we have what can properly be called propaganda, a rewriting of history with the conscious purpose of supporting a particular structure.

In the description given by Ronald Grimes we have a dramatic example of the use of ritual to legitimate a societal nomos. The complex ethos of Santa Fe, with its mixture of civic, ecclesial, and ethnic elements, is blended in the rites and pageantry of La Conquistadora and the Entrada, ceremonials in which the people participate, thereby affirming the whole order of their culture. For most authors,

11 Ibid., p. 157.
12 Ibid., p. 163.

78 / Law, Freedom, and Story

this is the primary function of rituals. Likewise, many students of religion see the sustaining of faith as the basic effect of liturgy.

Turner's Concept of Liminality

Let us now turn to the sociological analysis of the disruptive dynamic, the functions of anti-structure. We shall expect to find the socially disruptive as anti-structure and as counter-structure or counter-culture, which is analogous to Crossan's distinction between the purely parabolic and the counter-mythic. Turner is aware of both, although he has primarily written about the former.

In his discussion of social ceremonies, Turner employs "liminality" and "liminal," terms coined by Arnold van Gennep in his 1909 work, *Rites of Passage*. As his title suggests, van Gennep's basic interest was to present the rituals by which cultures, especially traditional ones, regularize the passage of individuals, and indeed of whole communities, from one status to another within the social structure, a classic example being the various forms of puberty rites. He recognized three moments, which he defined in serial terms as separation, margin, and reaggregation, or preliminal, liminal, and postliminal. Derived from the Latin *limen*, which means "threshold," the term "liminal" draws attention to van Gennep's belief that in these rites there is an important symbolic threshold through which one passes. It is a period when one is actually moving between stages and, consequently, not really part of any, and hence not part of the social structure in the fullest sense.

> The first phase, separation, comprises symbolic behavior signifying the detachment of the individual or group from either an earlier fixed point in the social structure or from an established set of cultural conditions (a "state"). *During the intervening liminal period, the state of the ritual subject . . . becomes ambiguous, neither here nor there, betwixt and between all fixed points of classification.* . . . In the third phase the passage is consummated and the ritual subject, the neophyte or initiand reenters the social structure, often, but not always at a higher status.[13]

Turner distinguishes two forms of ritual liminality. He terms the first "rituals of status elevation," corresponding to the emphasis in van Gennep, wherein the "traveller" is carried by the rite from one status to a higher one—from a boy to a man, from a commoner to a monarch—by passing through this liminal, non-status interlude. The

13 Turner, *Dramas, Fields, and Metaphors*, p. 232 (my emphasis).

second he calls "rituals of status reversal," ceremonies that usually have a corporate significance.[14] These are often cyclical or seasonal, marked by a time when certain persons momentarily transcend their low estate and are enabled to exercise authority over those who normally outrank them. For a moment they are liminal, with their actions taking them into otherwise forbidden behaviour outside the definitions of the social structure. Liminality, for van Gennep and initially for Turner, points to that moment in the ritual process when the individual or the group is lifted out of its formerly well-defined place in society.

> [The] ambiguous and indeterminate attributes [of liminal states] are expressed by a rich variety of symbols in many societies that ritualize social and cultural transitions. Thus, liminality is frequently likened to death, to being in the womb, to invisibility, to darkness, to bisexuality, to the wilderness and to an eclipse of the sun or moon.[15]

As employed by Turner, however, the concept of liminality is extended to cover "any condition outside or on the peripheries of everyday life,"[16] and so he broadens the term to cover two other forms of social relationship beyond that involved in rites of passage.[17] First is the state of "outsiderhood," where one in fact occupies a recognized or meaningful position within the social structure. This may be adopted voluntarily and on a temporary basis, or it may be a permanent lack of status ascribed to such individuals by those within the social structure. The priest, the shaman, the medium, as religious figures, are all outside the normal social structure, as are the culture-rejecting groups of modern hippies, hoboes, and gypsies. These are people who, by choice or designation, do not fit any place in the social structure, who live within the society as unclassified, non-status persons. They are liminal in the sense of standing outside the boundaries and definitions of everyday life. Turner distinguishes these from marginals, the people standing in two statuses within the structure, who consequently often experience a social tension. These include children of immigrants, people of mixed racial and ethnic background, and women who today assume roles not considered "feminine." They are not liminal regarding social structure itself; they occupy very definite places, or, more accurately, two niches in soci-

14 Victor Turner, *The Ritual Process* (Ithaca: Cornell University Press, 1969), p. 167.
15 Ibid., p. 95.
16 Turner, *Dramas, Fields, and Metaphors*, p. 47.
17 Ibid., pp. 231-34.

ety. In no way do they represent a rejection or dislocation of the structure. Psychologically, such persons may experience a sense of being caught between roles or statuses, the liminality of counter-identities which may be deeply disturbing to the individual but non-disruptive of the social order per se. (In his earlier writings, such as *The Ritual Process*, Turner uses "marginals" as equivalent to inferior status. However, let us consider the distinction which he now makes between them.)

In *Dramas, Fields, and Metaphors*, Turner cites "structural inferiority" as yet another form of liminality. By it he refers to those occupying the normally devalued or rejected places in society—the poor, the weak, the despised. Whether this be an imposed status, occupied semi-permanently, or one freely chosen on a temporary basis, such persons may exercise symbolic power. Witness Gandhi's *harijan*, his "children of God," and the *anawin* of the Hebrew prophets. All stand in religious tradition as potent symbols of protest against the social structure, and in anticipation of aspects of liminality yet to be discussed, they may also constitute powerful moments of communitas. In religious history we have St. Francis of Assisi and Prince Gautama, the Buddha, who voluntarily gave up wealth and status to become poor. Similarly, in literature we come upon Mark Twain's Negro slave Jim and the vagrant Huckleberry Finn, or read of Chekhov's poor Jewish fiddler, Rothschild's and Rousseau's noble savage. By identifying with the lowest and, in a sense, rejected elements of the structure one becomes anti-structural and subversive—especially when this is done by choice. Such people are liminal, not in standing outside all roles, but in occupying those that are peripheral. There they are often thought to possess some sort of magical power, magic itself being an expression of liminality.

Turner also recognizes corporate manifestations of liminality. Some, similar in tone to van Gennep's sense of transition, take the form of liminal periods in history. Like persons, societies may move from one fairly stable and well-established social order into a period of flux before a new order and a new set of social values can emerge. Turner believes that such periods reveal the same dual potential for positive and negative outcomes that generally characterizes the liminal. In addition, especially in post-industrial-revolutionary society, he recognizes, the "liminoid" in

> those genres of free-time activity, in which all previous standards and models are subjected to criticism, and fresh new ways of describing and interpreting sociocultural experiences are formulated. The first

of these forms are expressed in philosophy and science, the second in art and religion.[18]

The latter, however, have more the character of Turner's "outsiderhood" than of van Gennep's "transition." As previously mentioned, literature can use liminal figures from history or pure fiction as instruments to subvert the social order. Consequently, those committed to the status quo not infrequently legislate against "those who in industrial societies utilize such 'liminoid' genres as literature, the film, and higher journalism to subvert the axioms of the *ancien régime*."[19] If, as Turner suggests, we are at present in a liminal era, it is indeed important to consider the implications for theology. Is it enough to become simply another voice subverting the old order? This is a matter to which we shall return in later chapters.

Liminality and Social Change

Let me reiterate that one should expect to find two forms of liminal disruption: those that reject the social structure without offering a fully developed counter-structure, and those that articulate an alternative structure or counter-culture. Turner cites both.

Let us begin with the purely disruptive which offers no alternative. One can distinguish three forms of this "anti" sense, namely, liminal acts, liminal communities, and liminal literature. (The books of Jonah and Ruth which challenge the national exclusiveness of the Hebrews typify the latter, not to mention secular examples.) In a political context, the early literature developed in revolutionary movements may offer only an attack on the "corrupt" social order of the day without expounding a clear alternative. But Turner barely touches upon the literary form, being more interested in liminal acts and communities.

Referring to liminal acts, Turner focuses directly upon rituals and public ceremonials, thereby making a close tie with our previous discussion of narrative expressions. Here we see enacted narrative as a means of social disruption and change. A dramatic illustration is ritual abuse, a public ceremony in which "the high are obliged to accept the stigmata of the lowly and even to endure patiently the taunts of those who will become their inferiors as in the installation

18 Ibid., p. 15.
19 Ibid., p. 14.

rites of many African chiefs and headmen."[20] In *The Ritual Process*, he describes this activity among the Ndembu people of Zambia who practise the "reviling of the chief elect" as part of the ceremony for installation of a new monarch. The chief-to-be is harangued by a spokesman who cries:

> Be silent! You are a mean and selfish fool, one who is bad-tempered! You do not love your fellows, you are only angry with them! Meanness and theft are all you have! Yet here we have called you and we say you must succeed to the chiefmanship. Put away meanness, put aside anger, give up adulterous intercourse, give them up immediately.[21]

Coronation is preceded by a moral rebuke for the new king. Yet more drastic was the selection of a king for Gaboon where the unsuspecting choice was set upon by the general populace.

> They surrounded him in a dense crowd, and then began to heap upon him every manner of abuse that the worst mobs could imagine. Some spat in his face; some beat him with their fists; some kicked him; others threw disgusting objects at him; while those unlucky ones who stood outside, and could reach the poor fellow only with their voices, assiduously cursed him, his father, his mother, his sisters and brothers, and all his ancestors to the remotest generation. A stranger would not have given a cent for the life of him who was presently to be crowned.[22]

For Turner, this was actually part of a larger, structure-supporting ceremony, yet the act in itself constitutes a purely anti-structural event, stripping the monarch of all pretension to grandeur.

Because Turner's interest is primarily in the positive attributes of liminality, he includes another form of social leveling, that involved in the rites of passage, such as puberty. Abuse serves to strip away all status, like the humiliation of the king, but the purpose here is to ensure that the youth are properly socialized, adequately redefined into the social structure.

> The neophyte in liminality must be a *tabula rasa*, a blank slate, on which is inscribed the knowledge and wisdom of the group. . . . The ordeals and humiliations, often of a grossly physiological character, to which the neophytes are submitted represent partly a destruction of the previous status and partly a tempering of their essence in order to prepare them to cope with their new responsibilities.[23]

20 Ibid., p. 252.
21 Turner, *The Ritual Process*, p. 101.
22 Ibid., p. 171.
23 Ibid., p. 103.

Images of the indoctrination techniques of some cults are brought to mind by such descriptions. Less extreme would be the college initiation where the humiliation of freshmen serves to introduce the students to the mystique of their alma mater and to remind them of their lowly status. Again, in the context of the whole meaning of the rite, we have liminality as an instrument of structural reinforcement, anti-structure in the service of structure. A milder, institutionalized form of such liminality is found in the role of the court jester. Here was an individual set aside in both African and European courts, able to insult, challenge, or question the highest personages of the land. Turner describes an African example where the jester, frequently dwarfed or physically deformed (therefore, liminal?), was permitted to throw any noble who had offended him into the water.[24]

While ritual abuse involves the liminal in the sense of denying the social status of another, individuals themselves may choose to abandon attributes of status and act liminally. In many cases, such actions are undertaken out of allegiance to some alternative, communal ideal, but they are experienced by those adhering to the old order as a dramatic rejection and critique of the social structure. This may be shocking and provocative to the establishment. "A 'natural' or 'simple' mode of dress, or even undress in some cases, signalizes that one wishes to approximate the basically or merely human, as against the structurally specific by way of status or class."[25] In our own society the "flower children" deliberately rejected the macho and aggressive values of our culture. By their lifestyle—young men with long hair, wearing beads and flowers—they stood as enacted social protest and anti-structure. The anguished lament of the older generation, that one could no longer tell the boys from the girls, was a witness to the effectiveness of their assault on the role types taken for granted within the *ancien régime*. All this is liminal in stepping away from society's definitions.

One of the classic and most disturbing realms wherein liminal communities reject the social structure is in the area of sexual mores. This may take the form of either promiscuity or the total renunciation of sexual activity, marriage, and parenting. In either case, the result is a challenge to the structural assumptions of the culture in relating the sexes. Turner reminds us that it is not only in radical, secular, protest groups that such sexual revolutions have occurred, but also within the history of avowedly religious communities.

24 Ibid., p. 110.
25 Turner, *Dramas, Fields, and Metaphors*, p. 244.

> Thus some religious movements are similar to religious orders in abstaining from sexual activity, while others resemble some groups of hippies in breaking down sexual exclusiveness. Both attitudes toward sexuality are aimed at homogenizing the group by "liquidating" its structural divisions.[26]

One thinks of the rejection of traditional sexual roles by such religious groups as the Shakers, the Oneida community, and the Mormons.[27]

Religious movements, such as the strict, mendicant followers of St. Francis, constitute another expression that is essentially antistructural. One could hardly argue that they offered a counter-model for the community at large. An entire society cannot exist by begging from one another. Nevertheless, it was a fellowship that by its lifestyle expressed alternative values, and thereby implicitly challenged the accepted culture. St. Francis, Turner argues, seemed quite determined to keep his followers at the fringes of life, in a liminal state, in order to achieve a fuller humanness. Similarly, the cultural revolution in China, with the birth of the Red Guards, was a massive assault upon society, especially at those points where it was still deemed contaminated by the old, Confucian values. It was a social critique, serving a continual revolution, but not—per se—offering an alternative image.

With the recognition of such groups as the Mormons and Shakers, we move into the realm of the counter-cultural style of liminality. Here, in contrast to the essentially "anti" character of the Red Guards or the Franciscan Spirituals, one can list millenarian and utopian movements. The Fifth Monarchy Men, the Levellers, the Diggers, etc., in Cromwellian England, and thereafter, the Amish, the Mennonites, the Hutterites, the Shakers, and the Mormons—all constitute communities, some of long duration, who believed themselves to be expressing a more Christian social order and who thus stood as religious counter-cultures within Christendom. We have witnessed, in less religious terms, a host of counter-cultural movements in twentieth-century North America. Turner comments that "the Western urbanized hippies shared with many historical enthusiastic sects a desire to generalize and perpetuate their liminal and outsider condition."[28]

In keeping with his processual view of society, Turner articulates the process of social subversion in the interaction between culture

26 Ibid., p. 246.
27 Herbert W. Richardson, *Nun, Witch, Playmate* (New York: Harper & Row, 1971), pp. 129-36.
28 Turner, *Dramas, Fields, and Metaphors*, p. 261.

and counter-culture. It is interesting, in terms of the narrative focus of our overall study, that Turner sees this process as a "social drama" in which "conflicting groups and personages attempt to assert their own and deplete their opponents' paradigms," or, in our terms, to undermine the opposing nomos or structure.[29] The drama begins with a breach of normal social relations, signaled by some public act of non-compliance with a crucial norm leading to a heightening of tension. It ends in a redressive phase, producing either the domestication and incorporation of the counter-culture as a unit within the social structure or the recognition, in the larger society, of two opposing and competitive social structures that will now exist together. Turner cites the history of Sikhism in India. While the caste system is not all there is to Hinduism, it can be argued that a heterodox or anti-structural sect is one that is totally opposed to it, whereas orthodox sects involve an expansion upon that social system. Sikhism was by this definition, then, heterodox. It began as an attempt to annihilate the social, intellectual, and spiritual partitions of the Indian medieval world, including the abolition of its caste system. Eventually, by becoming organized into a complete religious system, it continued its opposition to Hinduism, no longer as anti-structure but now as counter-structure.[30] This example illustrates a point important to Turner and to the thesis of this work, namely, the dialectic between structure and anti-structure in human society.

In his study of Santa Fe, Grimes offers yet another example of social drama, this one involving the confrontation between counter-symbols. We have already made reference to Don Diego De Vargas as the ethnic hero of Spanish-American culture in Santa Fe. Opposing him as a counter-symbol is Reies Lopez Tijerina who stands as the champion of Indo-Hispanic culture in the struggle for social justice. The focusing issue is land grants and aboriginal rights. The debate involved the claim by Indo-Hispanics to large tracts of land that had been ceded to them originally by the Spanish kings, claims that subsequently had been confirmed by both Mexican and American governments. Over a period of time, however, these lands had been taken over by others and Tijerina became the centre of a popular movement to reclaim this lost patrimony. He is, clearly, a counter-structural element. He is also liminal in lifestyle, for dreams and visions are an important and guiding part of his experience. (They are, of course, liminal realities in our society. As a people we are used

---

29 Ibid., p. 15.
30 Ibid., pp. 275-79.

to organizing things in terms of rules and institutions, not in response to dreams and visions of individuals.) In lifestyle, then, Tijerina was outside the normal meanings, roles, and understandings of modern Santa Fe. He represents an intensely confronting counter-symbol in articulating a counter-interpretation of New Mexican history by proposing modifications in the social and economic structure, and also by incarnating a personal mode of existence that finds no acceptable place in the normal life patterns of the community. Tijerian and De Vargas have come to stand in the culture of New Mexico for two radically different and competing social structures, though each is an expression of Hispanic language and culture. Because of this commonality, in fact, they are more intensely in opposition as each claims to represent what is most truly and essentially Spanish. Grimes summarizes the situation as follows:

> Whereas Tijerina has many times challenged the legitimacy of civil authority, De Vargas is an instrument of king and religious hierarchy, the epitome of civil and religion authority. . . . Pushed to their caricatured limits, De Vargas is a symbol of royal, crusading imperialism while Tijerina is a symbol of militant, grass-roots revolution. De Vargas conquers and reconquers the land from the Indians; Tijerina wrests land from the Anglos. . . . De Vargas appeals to his banner of Our Lady, makes frequent use of rosaries and crosses, and incessantly shouts praises to the Blessed Sacrament [ecclesial social structure]; Tijerina appeals to dreams, visions, and basic human nature, that is, brotherhood awareness [liminality].[31]

While obviously not overthrowing the whole of Spanish-American culture in New Mexico, Tijerina embodies a counter-symbol, a counter-structure and, in that sense, is a subverting element without the social structure.

Mexico speaks as well of two competing figures, Our Lady of Guadalupe and Our Lady of Remedies, both of whose communities are centred in Mexico City. The clash between these competing symbols and their associated social structures goes back to the period of the Mexican struggles for independence in 1810. The insurgence, led by a priest, Miguel Hildalgo y Costilla, fought under the protection of Our Lady of Guadalupe, while the Spanish forces accepted Our Lady of Remedies as their spiritual commander, with the Spanish viceroy actually placing a marshal's baton in the hand of the diminutive figure. Turner comments:

31 Grimes, *Symbol and Conquest*, pp. 148-49.

> Perhaps because her image has so often been taken to the cathedral of Mexico City, Los Remedios has been linked with the upper bureaucracy of New Spain. She had certainly been connected with anti-revolutionary movements for some time.... Our Lady of Guadalupe, on the other hand, has always been associated with the insurgency of the common people.[32]

In modern Mexico both Los Remedios and Guadalupe are thought to offer protection to the people. Yet the distinction remain. Los Remedios characteristically is a white-faced virgin, associated with people as they participate in the paternalistic structures of a society, originally dominated by the European, Spanish whites, and later by Creoles with strong white affinities. Conversely, Guadalupe is portrayed with brown skin and, in her original appearance, spoke the native dialect. She is traditionally associated with the interests of the lower classes in Mexico.[33] Again we have two competing symbols, stories, and structures, though both are considered to manifest the concern of the Blessed Virgin.

Let me close this section with one final example of liminality to which Turner devotes considerable attention, namely, pilgrimage. It provides not only an interesting example of liminality drawn from religious history, particularly Christian and Muslim, but also a set of practices contrasting sharply with the structure-affirming or mythic rituals that Grimes details in the public ceremonies of Santa Fe. Writing with his wife Edith in *Image and Pilgrimage in Christian Culture*, Turner gives his attention to the study of liminality in Catholic Christianity which, as he says, he knows best. Here liminality does not express itself where he had anticipated—in the ordinary rituals of religion, the sacraments of baptism, the mass, etc. Rather, he finds it most powerful in pilgrimage, the journey to a sacred site, a holy shrine, that is distant from the pilgrims' normal place of abode and from their routine life and activities. He reminds us that for much of the period of Catholic Christendom the mass of people lived in fixed locations, especially in the feudal period. The sanctioning of pilgrimage allowed occasions for believers literally to move out of their place in the social structure and thus to experience, in a very significant way, the liminal.

> In societies with few economic opportunities for movement away from limited circles of friends, neighbors, and local authorities, all

---

32 Victor Turner and Edith Turner, *Image and Pilgrimage in Christian Culture* (New York: Columbia University Press, 1978), pp. 90-91.
33 Ibid., p. 92.

rooted alike in the soil, the only journey possible for those not merchants, peddlers, minstrels, jugglers, tumblers, wandering friars, or outlaws, or their modern equivalents, is a holy journey, a pilgrimage or a crusade. On such a journey one gets away from the reiterated "occasions for sin" which make up so much of the human experience of social structure.[34]

Moreover, in Christianity pilgrimage was not a prescribed ritual as it tends to be in Islam; it was a matter of free choice on the part of pilgrims, and that made it a negation of the obligatory character of social structure, of its imbeddedness. Turner remarks that "inside the Christian religious frame, pilgrimage may be said to represent the quintessence of voluntary liminality."[35] To go on a pilgrimage was to experience the liminal. To be sure, the meaning and raison d'être of pilgrimage was not to experience anti-structure. Indeed, the whole tradition became domesticated, finding its meaning within the structure of the Catholic faith. It became another means of salvation and the expression of an important form of human existence, which Turner calls communitas. (We shall discuss this later in detail.) Nevertheless, it remains basically a liminal experience with many of the associated characteristics. The Turners recognize four categories of pilgrimage but concentrate on modern pilgrimages, those that have arisen largely since Vatican I. These all manifest anti-structural character. To begin with, they are anti-modern in tone. Pilgrimage has always been associated with miracle, but this emphasis becomes particularly strong in relation to modern examples. There we find major stress upon such anti-cultural, anti-modern realities as visions and apparitions. The Turners point out that while the founding of medieval pilgrimages was often associated with apparitions, in many cases the stories of such appearances were not circulated until long after the founding of the cult itself. "In contrast, modern Marian pilgrimages begin quite explicitly with contemporary apparitions or other kinds of visions, and are subjected to close inquiry by the Church—and to ridicule by non-believers."[36] Accentuating the supernatural, modern pilgrimage finds itself a cultural reality in a liminal or anti-structural position, specifically repudiating the closed scientific universe that marks the nomos of modern secular culture.

Ronald Grimes contrasts the public rituals of the procession associated with La Conquistadora in New Mexico and the pilgrimages celebrating Our Lady of Guadalupe in Mexico. Processions are

34 Ibid., p. 7.
35 Ibid., p. 9.
36 Ibid., p. 174.

structural and non-liminal; pilgrimage is anti-structural and liminal. Unlike those involved in pilgrimage, persons in the Santa Fe processions undergo no strenuous activity, nothing that carries them away from the ordinary structures of life that they know; they are not called to go to strange and distant lands. The procession is, as we have seen, a celebration of the social structure. Consequently, as might be expected, the Santa Fe rituals make no appeal to the supernatural.

> Unlike the Virgin of Guadalupe, La Conquistadora does not represent a hierophany, if by this term one means a miraculous appearance of the holy, such as a vision or audition. Virtually no miracle tradition is connected with her. Many come to Santa Fe to visit her but few stories of healing or miracle surround her.[37]

Nomization and Liminality as Threat

The first step in the social process is the creation of a specifically human world. Social systems are man-made. Here Turner agrees with Berger:

> Natural systems, Znaniecki always argued, are objectively given and exist independently of the experience and activity of men. Cultural systems, on the contrary, depend not only for their meaning but also for their existence upon the participation of conscious, volitional human agents and upon men's continuing and potentially changing relations with one another.[38]

Peter Berger developed this idea at length in *The Sacred Canopy*. "Society," he wrote, "is a dialectic phenomenon in that it is a human product, and nothing but a human product, that yet continuously acts back upon its producer."[39] The individual is a product of society but, equally, society is a product of individuals. Hence, there is no predetermined world for people in the same sense that there is for animals, which sustain a tolerable harmony with their innate, "highly specialized and firmly directed drives."[40] The bee enters the bee world, but man as species must make a world—the specifically human world. Culture, then, represents an ordering or interpretation of reality, the provision of a framework or nomos within which one

37 Grimes, *Symbol and Conquest*, p. 37.
38 Turner, *Dramas, Fields, and Metaphors*, p. 32.
39 Peter Berger, *The Sacred Canopy* (Garden City, New York: Doubleday, 1967), p. 3.
40 Ibid., p. 5.

may live. Society is the guardian of that order and meaning, both through its social institutions and through the world-taken-for-granted into which its people are socialized. So, Berger can write: "To participate in the society is to share its 'knowledge,' that is, to co-inhabit its nomos."[41] The primary function of society, therefore, is nomization, the creation of a sociocultural, human structure within which we may live. In fact, it is impossible to live a human life apart from such a structure.

To fall outside structure is to know the powerful threat of chaos, meaninglessness, anomy. Liminality will naturally be interpreted by the community, especially by those strongly committed to the nomos, as a serious challenge. This is true whether or not such liminal groups see themselves as anomic. Actually, they may experience a more positive outcome in what Turner calls "communitas" and what I more broadly call the "transnomic." As Berger says, societies will devote considerable attention to the legitimation of their nomos. We see this constantly in individuals and institutions who function without question in allegiance to cultural definitions and values. At a more active level, the vast instrumentalities of socialization, especially the educational system, are vehicles for winning compliance from the young, new members. Beyond this, Berger mentions more drastic steps involving punitive actions against deviants.

Turner, however, describes a gentler and more effective way to protect social structure, namely, by domesticating the liminal, granting it a place within the structure, and thereby "deliminalizing" it. In tribal society, we have seen that the liminal appears primarily in the context of well-defined rituals that have as their ultimate goal the reaffirmation of structure and the shepherding of "pilgrims" during periods of social change. Turner remarks:

> In the liminality of tribal societies, traditional authority nips radical deviation in the bud. We find symbolic inversion of social roles, the mirror-imaging of normative secular paradigms; we do not find open-endedness, the possibility that the freedom of thought inherent in the very principal of liminality could lead to major reformulation of the social structure and the paradigms which program it.[42]

Structure and anti-structure are carefully combined in the one ceremony; iconoclasm exists within rituals that are heavy with icons. The seeming attacks on structure are themselves structured into situations

41 Ibid., p. 21.
42 Turner and Turner, *Image and Pilgrimage*, p. 3.

with prescribed times, forms, and limitations on their expression. They serve, in effect, as socially sanctioned occasions to transgress, let off steam, and by that very fact, they securely re-establish the social structure. "Cognitively," Turner writes, "nothing underlines regularity so well as absurdity or paradox. Emotionally, nothing satisfies as much as extravagant or temporarily permitted illicit behavior. Rituals of status reversal accommodate both aspects."[43] Rituals of role reversal and humiliation end by reaffirming the social structure they appear to attack. After an ecstatic experience of rebellion and even of communitas, one then returns to a purged but revitalized and reaffirmed social structure. The very act of liminal rebellion is now in the service of discipline: disorder has become an instrument of order.

Given the liminal character of pilgrimage as described by Turner, we are not surprised to find that occasionally it has met opposition from the guardians of the social structure, in this case from the ecclesial establishment. Turner mentions two ways in which it was seen as a threat and two corresponding responses. The older form was interpreted as an attack on the control and authority of the Church. Similar responses were forthcoming in other traditions.

> For this reason, orthodoxy in many religions tends to be ambiguous toward pilgrimage. The apparent capriciousness with which people make up their minds to visit a shrine, the rich symbolism and communitas quality of pilgrimage systems, the peripheral character of pilgrimage vis-à-vis the ritual or liturgical system as a whole, all make it suspect. Pilgrimage is too democratic, not sufficiently hierarchical.[44]

Pilgrimage also came to menace the established nomos because of the ludic or playful character of the liminal itself, a quality reflected in the clowning jester, masks, the dance, etc. Following the Industrial Revolution a sharp distinction came to be made between work and play, with a superior value given to the former. In this setting, the liminal as ludic, including its expression in pilgrimage, became a matter of concern. "Indeed, it is the ludic component which excited the wrath of many Christian critics of pilgrimage and perhaps prepared the way for the virtual abolition of pilgrimage in many Protestant lands."[45] (Here one may recall the movement cited earlier in modern psychotherapy to recover the Child, play, and fantasy as valued dimensions of humanness.)

43 Turner, *The Ritual Process*, p. 176.
44 Turner and Turner, *Image and Pilgrimage*, p. 31.
45 Ibid., p. 37.

In our own time we can think of the festival of Mardi Gras as an institutionalized form to let off steam so that people will then obey the traditional order and discipline of Lent. At a gentler level, Turner sees in the camaraderie, the egalitarianism, and the playfulness of the modern service club a domesticated communitas, a sterilized rejection of our competitive order of status and structure which, in effect, reinforces industrial-commercial society. Modern communities, no less than the traditional, seek to domesticate the liminal.

In summary, then, society inevitably involves the creation of an order, an interpretation, a nomos without which it cannot function, and it will, therefore, exercise all necessary steps to maintain that order. Liminality is usually seen as a threat to rationality and social structure, but Turner also expounds upon its creative possibilities within the whole social process. We shall now turn to these possibilities and relate them to the inevitability and necessity of the nomic.

Creative Liminality in the Social Process

To step outside the shared meanings and social values of a community can be a threatening experience. In Berger's terms, to leave the nomos of our people is to run the risk of chaos and anomy. Turner, however, articulates the positive potential of such a move: "When I speak of anti-structure... I really mean something positive, a generative center."[46] Here let us distinguish from within this generative centre the liminal as the basis for social critique and reformation, but also as a valuable state or experience in itself.

The potential to make individuals and communities aware of their structures and assumptions is part of the very nature of the liminal as conceived by Turner. When standing between statuses, we are inclined to become more self-consciously aware of the limitations and the relativity of our own social values, and to conceive of other possibilities.

> I see liminality as a phase in the social life in which this confrontation between "activity which has no structure," and its "structured results" produces in men their highest pitch of self-consciousness.... Liminality may have a pedagogical function in forcing those who have taken their culture for granted to rethink what they have hitherto taken to be its axioms and its "givens."[47]

46 Turner, *Dramas, Fields, and Metaphors*, p. 273.
47 Ibid., pp. 255-56.

Liminality offers the opportunity to overcome the automatic legitimation of culture. As Turner says in *The Ritual Process*, it "can be seen as potentially a period of scrutinization of the central values and axioms of the culture in which it occurs."[48] All cultures need a chance to step back from the social order and reflect upon it. The economic realities of tribal life seldom allowed time for philosophical or religious speculation. However, in the protracted periods of liminality associated with various rituals, occasion was provided for the reflection and self-awareness so essential for the growth of any society. There opportunity was afforded "to learn and speculate about what the tribe considers its 'ultimate things.'"[49] Similarly, in our own society which is so highly structured and, hence, so restrictedly liminal, Turner finds that we turn to cultural expressions of liminality in our poets and artists which serve this function of arousing self-consciousness.[50] Within the realm of theological thought, one thinks of the call for demystification and consciousness-raising ("conscientization") in liberation theologies, though here, perhaps, one encounters the liminality of inferior status rather than the liminality of the outsider. Looking to a more traditional religious form, Turner finds in modern Catholic pilgrimages another expression of liminality which provides an opening for reflection.

> In the scientific and technological age, pilgrimage is becoming what Geertz... has described as a "metasocial commentary" on the troubles of this epoch of wars and revolutions with its increasing signs of industrial damage to the natural environment. Like certain other liminoid genres of symbolic action elaborated in the leisure time of modern society, pilgrimage becomes an implicit critique of the lifestyle characteristic of the encompassing social structure.[51]

Liminality invites self-consciousness; it also encourages creativity. "Liminality is not only *transition* but also *potentiality*."[52] It was in liminal moments of traditional societies, in festivals, rituals, rites of passage, that an opportunity was given for free play of thought and emotion out of which grew new modes of conceptualizing the life, purpose, and values of a people. The "liminal" thinkers—the poets, writers, and religious prophets—are the true "legislators of mankind."[53] They are the ones who exercise imagination despite the

48 Turner, *The Ritual Process*, p. 167.
49 Turner, *Dramas, Fields, and Metaphors*, p. 259.
50 Ibid., p. 260.
51 Turner and Turner, *Image and Pilgrimage*, p. 38.
52 Ibid., p. 3.
53 Turner, *Dramas, Fields, and Metaphors*, p. 28.

limiting impact of structure, who challenge the restriction of thought by what is culturally "known to be true." As Frederick Buechner observes, "A child is apt to see certain things better than his elders, I think, because, less sure than they of what to *expect*, he is more apt than they to see what, actually though unexpectedly, *is*."[54] The words of this theologian find an echo in Turner. "The components of what I have called anti-structure, such as communitas and liminality, are the conditions for the production of root metaphors, conceptual archetypes, paradigms, models and the rest."[55]

If the liminal as anti-structure is the creative moment, what it creates most often is new structure. Turner, especially in *Dramas, Fields, and Metaphors*, stresses the dialectical relationship between structure and anti-structure. As he says, Max Weber, in his treatment of charisma, has observed the tendency for anti-structure to become domesticated and absorbed into the structural. Social transformations often begin in liminal figures, the shaman, the prophet, the revolutionary, the charismatic leader, who exercise a personal authority and offer a transforming critique of their society. Over a period of time this authority, residing in the charismatic power of the leader, becomes transformed into traditional authority, residing in social institutions, especially religious ones. Then it often becomes even more formally and rigidly structural as it is replaced by legal authority. While for Weber the dynamic force in social history is charismatic authority, the fate of charisma is to become routinized.

Turner gives a number of examples of this interesting phenomenon, citing some from religious history. We have already explored his view of Sikhism, which began as an anti-structural critique of Hinduism but gradually became a counter-structure. As for Confucianism, it distinguishes between *li* and *jen*, *li* being the customs and rules that regulate society and *jen* a spontaneous dynamic of love, goodness, and human relationships. It emphasizes the importance of both and their relationship to each other. Moreover, Turner claims that we would not grossly distort their meanings were we "to translate *jen* as 'the sentiment of humankindness or for humanity,' and its social expression as communitas, while *li* is not so far from what I have called structure."[56] This dialectic does not always lead immediately to synthesis but may, in fact, find expression in the

54 Frederick Buechner, "All's Lost, All's Found," *The Christian Century*, March 12, 1980, p. 282.
55 Turner, *Dramas, Fields, and Metaphors*, p. 50.
56 Ibid., p. 284.

institutionalizing of the two moments, the structural and the anti-structural. The liminal lifestyle of St. Francis, with its strict call for poverty, proved difficult as the model for a large and enduring religious order. There was an inevitable tension between the intimacy and spontaneity of communitas in St. Francis and the requirements of social organization. Consequently, his followers split into two groups, the Conventuals who relaxed the rigours of the saint's lifestyle in the service of organization and the Spirituals who insisted upon a *usus pauper* and lived in a manner that was structurally more difficult.

Turner observes that the very success of a pilgrimage naturally leads to a large number of participants, necessitating the organization of the event at the cost of some of its original spontaneity and liminality. "Conceptual and institutional structuration of penitential pilgrimage prepared the way for the demise of the pilgrimage system in its high medieval form, for it no longer represented communitas, social anti-structure."[57] One can view the Reformation originally as an anti-structural movement. From its inception it appealed to a structure that the reformers construed as the true order and community of the early Church. In time, however, it became as structured as the Roman Catholicism it assailed. The initial freedom of its theological spirit was converted into a new scholasticism. Inevitably, there appears to be an interaction between structure and anti-structure, with the latter constantly under pressure to become a new structure. More precisely, we find a dialectic of structure, anti-structure, and counter-structure. It would be a misinterpretation of Turner's thesis, however, were we to see this as a tragic process, for both structure and anti-structure are necessary to the health of societies. One should oppose, therefore, attempts to subordinate communitas and the liminal to the rigours of structure and, likewise, efforts to establish some formless reality that rejects all social differentiations. We must resist not only the "bureaucratic *ubermensch* who would like to array the whole world of lesser men in terms of hierarchy and regimentation," but also "the puritanical levelers who would abolish all idiosyncratic differences between man and man."[58]

The task of any culture isto find a proper balance between structure and anti-structure. The great religious systems, Turner reminds us, have always sought finally to harmonize communitas and order. The New Testament image of the body of Christ carries

57 Turner and Turner, *Image and Pilgrimage*, p. 196.
58 Turner, *Dramas, Fields, and Metaphors*, p. 268.

something of this harmony. Yet there is more here than the balancing of two necessary elements in human experience, of polar opposites. We have a true dialectical relationship where the reality of each is informed and infused by the other, thereby energizing the development of human communities. "Man is both a structural and an anti-structural entity, who *grows* through antistructure and *conserves* through structure."[59] (The parallels here with Tillich's discussion of Protestant principle and Catholic substance are obvious.) The liminal opens the door to self-transcendence and creativity, enabling a society to conceptualize alternatives, to transcend its traditions and choose new options. But always and inevitably, if a people are to survive, they will again seek out a structure, a new nomos and social order that capture the spirit of their liminal insights.

Positive Liminality

As mentioned earlier, Berger in *The Sacred Canopy* emphasizes the negative consequences of rejecting the societal definition of reality. Anomy is identified as a major peril for humanity. Turner, by contrast, regards the anti-structural moment as one of dual potential, as crisis in the medical sense, with the possibility of positive as well as negative results. To step outside the nomos, not simply in that moment of self-awareness and critical judgment, but even radically to do so, does not inevitably invite chaos. On the other hand, one has no assurance that the abandonment of structure guarantees a positive experience. For the individual, it may result only in personal confusion and a loss of identity; for a society, it may end in chaos, "either a Hobbesian war of all against all, or an existentialist anarchy of individuals."[60] Nonetheless, the positive potential remains. Thus Turner asserts that "liminality often provides favorable conditions for communitas."[61] Outside nomos lies not only anomy but also communitas. (With a slightly different emphasis, I might employ a variant of Tillich's understanding of the transmoral conscience, asserting that one can become anti-structural either anomically or transnomically. I suggest, in the following chapter, that communitas is a transnomic phenomenon.) The rituals and symbols involved in the expression of liminality usually reflect this dual potential. The point is that one can find a latent positive beyond structure; that is what Turner has highlighted.

59   Ibid., p. 298.
60   Ibid., p. 285.
61   Ibid.

Communitas as positive, as transnomic, is a potentiality within the very nature of the liminal, not simply when that liminality is achieved through some specifically controlled ceremony. The very dissolution of structure may provide an opportunity for the spontaneous creation of the intensified human relationships that is communitas. Turner cites the escape of British forces from France in 1940 when the breakdown of organization among the Allied armies was followed by a spontaneous liberation of human feelings and commitments, producing that flotilla of tiny boats in the Channel, known as the "miracle of Dunkirk." He does not deny that such occasions are also marked by angst and anomy. Contrasting social processes may operate in one and the same situation. He merely maintains that "[s]tructure's breakdown may be communitas' gain."[62]

Communitas, avowedly, is a positive state or condition for human existence. It is not merely *anti*-structure; it has a content. (There is some inconsistency at times in Turner's terminology. Occasionally, he seems to contrast communitas with liminality. Thus, for example, he writes, "What I call liminality, the state of being in between successive participations in social milieux . . . is not precisely the same as communitas."[63] Yet in other instances, he uses the term liminality synonymously with anti-structure, distinguishing within that term the purely anti-structural, which is nothing but the rejection of structure—the purely parabolic—and social anti-structure, which is a form of communal life with liminal quality. The latter is more than the rejection of structure; it is an alternative social expression.) In short, communitas is liminality, not merely as anti-structure but as a social style. It is the non-structured community. Hence, in many situations where people seek to create communitas, they begin with a very specific attack upon, or destruction of, tradition. Whereas social structure implies a society with a system of differentiated roles and relatively fixed positions, communitas suggests a homogeneous, undifferentiated form of human relationships. Turner gives a detailed definition, in his book on pilgrimages, where he speaks of communitas as "social antistructure":

> [Communitas or social antistructure is a] relational quality of full unmediated communication, even communion, between definite and determinate identities, which arises spontaneously in all kinds of groups, situations, and circumstances. . . . It is a liminal situation which combines the qualities of lowliness, sacredness, homogeneity,

62 Ibid., p. 251.
63 Ibid., p. 52.

and comradeship. . . . It does not merge identities; it liberates them from conformity to general norms, though this is a necessarily transient condition if society is to continue to operate in an orderly fashion.[64]

Turner is critical of the existentialist philosophers who fail to differentiate between the "liminalities of solitude and communitas."[65] Rejecting, seemingly, the inauthenticity of structure, Heidegger and others make the incorrect assumption that social existence cannot be genuine since it is always defined by things extraneous. Unfortunately, they overlook the communal relationship that transcends the confining and—for existentialists—inauthenticating impact of structures. They miss the possibility of social anti-structure or communitas.

Turner asserts that communitas is holistic, involving the total person in relationship to others, while social structure is fundamentally cognitive, involving ways of conceptualizing relationships. (I shall be maintaining shortly that communitas also involves a different kind of conceptualization or cognition.) While asserting that Martin Buber cannot be called a social scientist, Turner finds, in his conception of the I-Thou, an intuitive insight into communitas as a relationship of "being no longer side by side (and, one might add, above and below) but *with* one another. . . . [A] turning to, a dynamic facing of, the others, a flowing from *I* to *Thou*."[66] Communitas entails the immediate I-Thou encounter between whole persons in their uniqueness, rather than in terms of social role status. Being realistic and given the practicalities of living, we cannot possibly exist solely and continuously in a state of communitas. Human groupings require ordering. Once more Turner recognizes a dialectic between the immediacy of communitas and the mediacy of structure. But the state of communitas is not simply a necessary instrument for the reform of society. It represents an ideal. As a constant experience, it is, in Reinhold Niebuhr's phrase, another "impossible possibility." Yet for Turner, the moment of communitas is the highest expression of humanness.

Humanity needs anti-structure not merely to purge what is, but also to cherish in itself. It is essential that we nurture both structure and anti-structure, and insofar as ritual reflects the two, it is a most effective instrument. It offers concrete meaning, the values and defi-

64 Turner and Turner, *Image and Pilgrimage*, p. 250.
65 Turner, *Dramas, Fields, and Metaphors*, p. 54.
66 Martin Buber, quoted in Turner, *The Ritual Process*, p. 127.

nitions of a society, but simultaneously invites one to transcend these concrete meanings. Ritual, like story, is *mythoparabolic*.

> Both structure and anti-structure are represented in the concrete imageries and acts of the ritual process in tribal and peasant societies.... [In their non-verbal symbols] structure and anti-structure have not become as yet generalized into opposed ideological positions, well adapted to political manipulation, but the metaphors of iconoclasm exist *within* the text of ceremonies heavily endowed with icons.[67]

In Crossan's terminology, parabolic metaphors exist within structures heavy with mythic meaning.

The state of communitas mirrors a deep sense of generic bond between people as individuals and a sentiment for "humankindness" which is more than some mere herd instinct. It is truly to be alive![68] Symbolically expressed as Eden, paradise, Utopia, communitas is the goal of religious and, not infrequently, political activity. It is visualized as a community of free and equal comrades.[69]

Some of the social phenomena that we have already analyzed as parabolic should now be considered as communitas. St. Francis, seeking to keep his followers in a liminal state, was not only consciously rejecting material wealth but also attempting to foster this ideal. In the modern secular scene, the hippies sought in their own way to reach this goal. "They stress personal relationships rather than social obligations, and regard sexuality as a polymorphic instrument of immediate communitas rather than as the basis for an enduring structured social tie."[70] Time and again, Turner underlines the power of communitas associated with pilgrimage, an experience providing "a carefully structured, highly valued route to a liminal world where the ideal is felt to be real, where tainted social persona may be cleansed and renewed."[71] Not only is communitas the ultimate religious objective, it is also a necessary element in the survival of structure. For Turner, rituals in their structural capacity are necessary defenses against anomy and chaos, fulfilling a mythic or nomizing function, but they can do this only "where there is already a high level of communitas in the society that performs the ritual, the sense that a basic generic bond is recognized beneath all its hierarchical and

67 Turner, *Dramas, Fields, and Metaphors*, pp. 294-95.
68 Turner, *The Ritual Process*, p. 128.
69 Turner, *Dramas, Fields, and Metaphors*, pp. 237-38.
70 Turner, *The Ritual Process*, pp. 112-13.
71 Turner and Turner, *Image and Pilgrimage*, p. 30.

segmentary differences and oppositions."[72] One can argue not only that we have a dialectic between structure and communitas to critique and reform culture, but also that we must always have an underlying foundational experience of communitas for humane society to survive at all. (I recall the thought, expounded in my earlier work, that apart from a prior sense of commitment to community, without some feeling of allegiance and fellowship, there is no true morality. The moral imperative, apart from communitas, can operate only as naked fear, not truly as a moral category.)

Let us now consider communitas and structure in relation to the bicameral mind. Turner remarks that "the liminal situation of communitas is heavily invested with structure of a kind. But this is not a social structure . . . [rather] one of symbols and ideas, an instructional structure."[73] Communitas can be conceived of as an ordering of life, not in terms of social relationships, but of symbols, myths, and images that draw one into a deeper and fuller relationship with reality. All this may have strong parallels, I suggest, with right and left hemisphere conceptualization and logic. Turner, for example, draws attention to the distinction in Zen Buddhism between *prajna* and *vijnana*—roughly equivalent to intuition and discursive reasoning—and remarks that these two concepts "are rooted in the contrasting social experiences that I have described respectively, as 'communitas' and 'structure.'"[74] He adds that "*prajna* . . . would be the source of 'foundation'—or root metaphors, since these are eminently synthetic; on them *vijnana* does its work of discriminating the structure of the root metaphor."[75] The parallels here with the distinctions between right and left hemisphere thought are obvious. Moreover, I suggest that *prajna* or communitas thought corresponds to the experience of grasping intuitively, or even experiencing, one's fundamental vision of reality, one's faith, whereas *vijnana*, structural thought, submits such a vision to analytic criticism in its concrete application to living. Expressed in different metaphors, communitas knows the reasoning of the heart, structure the reasoning of the mind. Moreover, discussing these contrasting forms of conceptualization, Turner suggests that behind them may lie "a fundamental structure of human mentality or even of the human brain itself."[76] Communitas brings us into a state

72 Turner, *Dramas, Fields, and Metaphors*, p. 56.
73 Ibid., p. 240.
74 Ibid., p. 46.
75 Ibid., p. 48.
76 Ibid., pp. 240-41.

of being in which the whole mind and especially the right hemisphere, which our society and its educational systems tend to neglect, are called into play, thereby enabling us to reach a fuller understanding, which is yet another reason for instructing new adults into the deepest truths and mysteries of their people while in the liminal state.

> In order to implant this instructional structure firmly in the minds of neophytes it seems necessary that they should be stripped of structural attributes. . . . Men who are heavily involved in jural-political, overt, and conscious structure are not free to meditate and speculate on the combinations and oppositions of thought; they are themselves too crucially involved in the combinations and oppositions of social and political structure and stratification. . . . But in ritual liminality they are placed, so to speak, outside the total system and its conflicts. . . . Life as a series and structure of status incumbencies inhibits the full utilization of human capacities.[77]

Much that modern psychology would say has been repressed in the unconscious finds symbolic expression in many liminal situations, especially in rituals.[78] Again, ritual provides opportunities in the moment of communitas to get in touch with fuller dimensions of one's being. Consequently, in ritual, pilgrimage, and liminality generally the playful, the ludic, the Child is released and nurtured.

In summary, I have not been striving for an exhaustive survey of sociological thought on societal processes, but have concentrated only on those elements, especially in the work of Victor Turner, that are most useful for elucidating the issues of interest to this study. I believe that the primary contribution he makes is in developing the positive contribution of the liminal or anti-structural in the social dialectic. He sees both a critical and a creative function in continually reforming the social nomos, and a reality with values, in and for itself, that which he speaks of as communitas. In setting out this positive function of the liminal, he has developed the dialectical relationship between structure and anti-structure, between the ordering and disordering elements in cultural life, be it social structure, personality development or religious faith. Two further elements are found in his work which receive less attention but which are suggestive parallels with earlier parts of our study. One is the recognition of the dual function of ritual (enacted story) both as a means of affirming and transmitting a social structure, and as a ceremonial vehicle disruptive of structure. Rituals may have either as their primary aim. It would

77 Ibid., pp. 241-42.
78 Ibid., pp. 256-58.

seem, however, that as enacted, they always carry both potentials. The disruptive, challenging rituals such as the shaming of the chief-elect also help to regularize the process of succession and to stabilize society. Conversely, though, such nomos-affirming ceremonies as the Entrada, by inviting the playful participation of the folk—civic dignitaries dressed up in ancient costume, etc.—set free something of the liminal and disruptive spirit. Finally, there are strong similarities between the nature of ritual experience and the playful, childlike and imaginative which we have identified as positive factors in therapy.

5
The Dual Transcending of Law

As mentioned earlier, this study arose out of two strands of activity. First was my growing interest in religious narrative, the verbal telling and ritual acting out of stories, as a major medium for the presentation and preservation of faith. This whetted a desire to examine the dynamics of storytelling within that process. Since religious traditions have always offered some sort of salvation, fulfillment, or wholeness, I turned to the place of narrative in psychotherapy and social transformation, seeking clues to its role in religion. The second strand of activity was an attempt to reflect further on the material in an earlier work, *Ethical Confrontation in Counseling*. Though by and large well received, that study drew criticism from some readers who saw in it—despite my conscious and declared opposition to such understandings—a moralistic stance. It seemed to me that, for these critics, law was, by definition, legalism, moralism, bondage, restriction. This issue was but a secondary consideration, especially during the early phases of the present reflections which were actually begun before I received these comments.

The previous three chapters outline some of the materials examined in relation to the dynamics of storytelling. We started with a New Testament study of the parables of Jesus, offering the thesis that storytelling, by its very nature, provides a structure or meaning within which one can live and yet which invites the hearer to play with or fantasize within that meaning, and thus to disrupt or challenge it to some degree. I stated that storytelling is inevitably a mythoparabolic experience, and further suggested that by examining the use of narrative modes in therapy, we would again find this double function. Stories are used self-consciously in some therapy as a way of offering specific contents, understandings of reality. Often this amounts to a subtle presentation that slips past the ordinary, defensive mechanisms of the counselee. In other circumstances, storytelling, in the form of fantasy, becomes a medium that rejects any attempt to define precise meaning, particularly any attempt to capture *the* meaning of the tale. We have reason to argue that therapy may reach its highest moment when one transcends structure, order, identity, when, according to D. W. Winnicott, the therapist and patient can play together. Subsequently, we pursued the structuring and disruptive function of narrative in terms of the relationship between social rituals and social order—primarily in the work of Victor Turner. We found the potential of narratives and rituals both to reaffirm the world-taken-for-granted and to disrupt it. Turner also suggests that the most fully human social experience, which he calls communitas, requires moving beyond structure. While Berger implies that outside nomos is anomy, Turner looks beyond nomos to the creative possibility of this fuller humanness.

We have here a series of reflections that focus upon the nomic or order and the anti-nomic or anti-order. (The latter has a rather awkward ring, but "disorder" implies a negative, anomic character which I do not necessarily intend.) For Crossan, this is expressed as myth and parable, with parable offering a double possibility—either the complete disruption of the mythos or an opening to a deeper reality which is the Transcendent, the Divine. In therapy, we find the relationship between order as identity or perspective and the challenge to such order which can end with the normless and lost individual, as in Erikson's identity diffusion, or the zombie-like state of prisoners completely disoriented in concentration camps, as described by Bettelheim.[1] Yet such challenge can also lead to the freedom which enhances therapy and fuller growth. Finally, the same pattern occurs between social structure and anti-structure, where the latter invites either to social chaos or to communitas. Central to what I believe to be a major factor in the religious potential of narrative

---

1   Bruno Bettelheim, *The Informed Heart* (Glencoe, Ill.: Free Press, 1960), pp. 147-50.

looms a new, expanded articulation of the relationship between law and gospel, which may meet the concerns of those suspecting a new cryptomoralism in my previous work. Should this be true, it is a happy and serendipitous consequence, the power of narrative and its theological implications being my primary concern.

With reference to law and gospel, we must distinguish a twofold relationship. The discussion in *Ethical Confrontation in Counseling* primarily focused upon the first, possibly encouraging some to see in it covert legalism. Continuing the style of the former work, I shall draw quite openly upon theological discussions and symbols, seeking at the same time to elucidate their psychosocial meaning, which remains valid whether or not one accepts their full theological superstructure. I hope that the non-theological reader will pursue the argument for yet one more chapter, not allowing the language immediately to end conversation. (Perhaps the different phrasing may serve helpfully— in a parabolic manner.)

Law, Gospel, and the Transmoral (Works vs Grace)

Law, in each of the two forms we shall examine, has the potential to produce a form of bondage. In the first case, it is bondage to good works, the tyranny of moral demands—be they those made upon us by others or those exercised by our own ideal. Psychotherapy has unveiled the dreadful wrath of the moral law, the living hell of individuals who know no "right to be," apart from fulfilling their own or their community's ethical code. Such is the character of a moralistic conscience. Obviously, if the demands are experienced as a standard of action imposed upon us by another, then we are inevitably caught in a moral tyranny, for our freedom to be in that relationship, our acceptance by the other, depends upon our having fulfilled the demand—or so we believe. Such was the essential character of the conscience described by Freud in his concept of the superego. Yet even if we are guided by our own ideals, if we are governed not by guilt, by the fear of failure, but by moral aspiration and an unambivalent striving for desired standards, we may still exist under a terrible moral tyranny, denying ourselves the right to be. Thus it finally does not matter whether we live in fear of rejection by another, of "the hangman," as Luther phrased it, or whether we fear self-rejection, the loss of self-worth because we have failed our own norms, for in either case, morality, ethics, law stands as a source of dreadful and debilitating tyranny in the lives of men and women. This was the essence of law in the experience and understanding of Luther, revealed in his own battles to fulfill the demands of a holy God and to avoid his wrath. I think it fair to say that Luther in his early life functioned under a negative conscience, trembling before an imposed demand. Modern therapy has found this same reality in the truncated lives of people who acquire no sense of self-worth other than through moral achievement. Freedom, in this context, requires breaking out of bondage to works, to ethical accomplishment, in short, to law so conceived. As Paul Tillich puts it, "Indeed, it is impossible *not* to transcend the moral conscience because it is impossible to unite a *sensitive* and a *good* conscience."[2]

Tillich describes the quality of conscience liberating us from the tyranny of moral ideals as "transmoral." The transmoral conscience is one that seeks to establish the individual's right to be, prior to and apart from any moral achievement. It offers a security beyond ethical accomplishment. This was precisely the ethical and psychological reality that the reformers were seeking to describe in their proclamation of justification by grace through faith, or more simply, justification by faith. The ultimate grounds for our security depends, not on what we do, but upon what God has graciously done. Our right to be is a free gift, not a reward to be earned. Luther developed this in his contrast between active and passive righteousness, the former being that which one seeks to obtain as a personal achievement. He considered it both an impossibility and a denial of the love and glory of God. The Christian should seek only passive righteousness, the free gift bestowed apart from any fulfilling of the law. "Thus I abandoned myself from all active righteousness, both mine own and of God's law, and embrace only that passive righteousness, which is the righteousness of grace, mercy and forgiveness of sins."[3] Emil Brunner expressed the same sentiment in this present century: "This is what faith means: to *know* that one is thus "born again," to accept life as a gift and righteousness as something outside oneself."[4] One can express this in both theological and psychological contexts:

> We are ultimately freed from the tyranny of our own ideals only as these are founded in the God who gives Himself to the sinner out of a

2 Paul Tillich, *The Protestant Era* (Chicago: University of Chicago Press, 1948), p. 149.
3 Martin Luther, *A Commentary on St. Paul's Epistle to the Galatians* (Westwood, New Jersey: Fleming H. Revell, 1953), p. 23.
4 Emil Brunner, *The Divine Imperative* (Philadelphia: Westminster Press, 1947), p. 77.

love which is grounded in His own nature and not in our achievement. In psychological terminology, we are only secure from the tyranny of conscience if that conscience recognizes our right to be (including the security of our relation to one who is the source of moral authority) prior to any ethical achievement.[5]

We cannot but see strong parallels between the psychodynamic reality conveyed in the Reformation doctrine of justification by faith and the modern experience of the therapeutic power of acceptance, which Carl Rogers refers to as "unconditional positive regard." Indeed, Paul Tillich suggests that modern theology had to learn again, from psychotherapy, the full meaning and power of grace, forgiveness, and the acceptance of the unacceptable. Even as we must experience free acceptance in order to grow in therapy, so also, in the realm of social ethics and the struggle for societal transformation, we need to grant the right to be to those persons whom we would call to new styles of living, new value commitments. It may be nearly impossible for the whites of South Africa, for example, to contemplate any change if they are required first to admit that they are despicable and that they must earn acceptability in the eyes of the social reformer.

To be sure, there is a kind of freedom that occurs simply by denying the validity of moral claims altogether, by asserting that we are free to do just as we wish, seeing no judgments apart from expediency, no place for an ethical imperative. Such, I have argued earlier, is personally and socially destructive and, finally, therapeutically ineffective. We cannot escape the moral dimensions of life simply by pretending that they do not exist. Freedom cannot really be found in denying the necessity for ethical responsibility.

The transmoral conscience, then, grants us the right to be apart from ethical achievement, apart from having become good. Nevertheless, it does not deny the reality and validity of moral claims. Tillich was at pains to remind us of the danger of the transmoral conscience so easily ceasing to be transmoral and achieving a false liberty by becoming amoral. We must hold our free right to be concomitant with a recognition of the continuing validity of the moral imperative. Actually, it was the misreading of justification by faith as a legal fiction, abolishing the moral imperative, which led Catholic theologians to oppose it so vigorously. Precisely to avoid such misunderstanding Calvin dealt first with law as a continuing and valid aspect in the life of faith, the so-called third use.

5 Hoffman, *Ethical Confrontation in Counseling*, p. 97.

The transmoral conscience remains *trans*moral, not amoral, only if the experience of justification by faith is held in creative tension with the call to sanctification. To be sure, in keeping with the concept of free justification, even this regeneration is the unmerited gift of God, divine grace producing the transformation in us. The individual still senses the call to struggle, to express and incarnate more fully the moral ideals to which allegiance is given. Though one is freely forgiven, Luther warned, "let him know that with the burden laid down, God's warfare is on, and he takes on another burden for God against the Devil and his own domestic vices."[6] The tension between justification and sanctification was reconciled for the reformers in their experience of faith. Such faith bound them in a relationship with the one who, while accepting them without reservation, drew them towards himself in a process of personal transformation. So Calvin wrote, "Christ justifies no one whom he does not at the same time sanctify."[7] The full experience of the transmoral conscience conceived in these theological images involves being bound in a relationship of trust and joy with a morally alluring graciousness, with a holy *and* loving God. The transmoral carries us beyond the moral law which demands achievement in exchange for the right to be, yet it does not deny the validity of the moral claim *in se*. Thus Tillich writes:

> A conscience may be called "transmoral" which judges not in obedience to a moral law but according to the participation in a reality which transcends the sphere of moral commands. A transmoral conscience does not deny the moral realm, but it is driven beyond it by the unbearable tensions of the sphere of law.[8]

What, then, is the place of law in the life of faith? To begin with, law functions within the economy of God as a preparation for gospel, as a necessary first stage in the life of human society, that which the reformers termed its first and second uses. At this level it has, for Luther, its proper functions. The first use maintains a minimal level of social order through restraining the evil impulses of unredeemed humanity. Without law in this sense, all the higher achievements of culture would be impossible, including the freedom to preach the gospel, and too often people would fall into a totally dissolute style of life. Law, in a second spiritual use, encounters men and women as an

---

6 Martin Luther, quoted in Gordon Rupp, *The Righteousness of God* (London: Hodder and Stoughton, 1953), p. 182.
7 John Calvin, *Institutes of the Christian Religion* (Philadelphia: Westminster Press, 1960), III.11.1.
8 Paul Tillich, *The Protestant Era*, p. 145.

intensified awareness of the moral claim and of their own moral failure, driving the unrepentant into a state of despair and shattering the hope for active righteousness in those whom God would save. It opens them to the experience of passive righteousness, to God's love for them, though they are sinners. Law, for Luther, in these two ways was fulfilling its proper function in the plan of God, yet this was not the fullest expression of the divine nature. Law, in this sense, is the manifestation of God's wrath, his "strange work." The reformers allowed such a place for it in the life of the faithful because the latter are never purely regenerate in this world. Thus it continues to curb their excesses, to quicken their sense of need and inadequacy, all as a preparation for the gospel. Ultimately, however, when it is so conceived, not only are law and gospel polarities within the religious life, but they are also totally opposed orientations of the self. Where there is gospel, law can no longer be. One trusts either in the grace of God or in one's own achievements. In this spirit, Luther proclaims that "Christ . . . is no Moses, no lawgiver, no tyrant."[9] Either we are free or we are in bondage. Law means bondage, even when it serves a useful, proleptic function. Gospel proclaims the glorious freedom of the children of God. This sharp contrast, found in the Reformation discussion, has tended to leave Protestant theology with a very deep sense that law *in se* is inherently contrary to gospel. This may well have caused a failure to distinguish, as quite separate and distinct, another tension between the two—a true polarity without opposition, wherein law has a continuing function and may itself be seen, in Luther's phrase, not as God's "strange" but "proper work." Now let us turn to a fuller examination of law in the life of faith, that which the reformers called its third use.

Law, Gospel, and the Transnomic (Structure and Anti-Structure)

In our second relationship between law and gospel, law no longer connotes a demand for achievement prior to one's right to be, but now is seen as a necessary, guiding reality. The distinction here is between law in its first and second uses and law in its third use. After the experience of grace, after the birth of faith, after the liberating awareness of free justification by God, continuing in the life of faith is law as a form of guidance, even in Luther's theology where it has been wrongly denied by some. According to Luther, "The law is

---

9 Luther, *Galatians*, p. 52.

given besides and above reason, to be a light and a help to man and to show him what he ought to do, and what to leave undone."[10] He offers, on more than one occasion, an exposition of the Ten Commandments as spiritual direction for the life of faith. It would be contrary, indeed, to the spirit of the reformers to see law at this point primarily as a code or list of behaviours. Rather, it was for them an instrument to bring people into a fuller consciousness of that which is our true norm, namely, Jesus Christ. Law could be said to offer a model for Christian identity, the image of him we are called to follow, the one "whose pattern we ought to express in our life."[11] It is, then, an ordering, structuring reality. Moreover, psychologically it is a matter no longer of imposition but of aspiration. As Calvin puts it, the Christian longs to obey God. Luther in his more vivid language writes: "But, to fulfill the law, is to do the things which the law commands with a joyful, glad and free heart; that is, spontaneously and willingly to live unto God, and do good works, as though there were no law at all."[12]

Given the strong emphasis upon law in its first two uses, most Protestant Christians have tended to equate it with the demand for achievement, thereby overlooking law as guidance, order, structure, or in our terms, nomos. We tend to view it through what we assume to be the experience of Luther and the Paul of Galatians, but are apt to miss this other fundamental sense of law as teaching or instruction, akin to the Hebrew torah.

> The Septuagint rendered the Hebrew *torah* by the Greek *nomos* ("law") probably in the sense of a living network of traditions and customs of a people. The designation of Torah by *nomos*, and by its Latin successor *lex* (whence, "the law"), has historically given rise to the sad misunderstanding that Torah means legalism.[13]

In the same spirit, E. P. Sanders argues that we should see the Hebrew faith as expressing "covenantal nomism."

> The 'pattern' or 'structure' of covenantal nomism is this: (1) God has chosen Israel and (2) given the law. The law implies both (3) God's promise to maintain the election and (4) the requirement to obey.

10 Ibid., p. 184.
11 Calvin, *Institutes of the Christian Religion*, III.6.3.
12 Martin Luther, "Preface to the Epistle of Paul to the Romans," in Henry Cole (ed.), *Select Works of Martin Luther* (London: W. Simpkin and R. Marshall, 1826), vol. 1, p. 205.
13 Warren Harvey, "Torah: Nature and Purpose," *Encyclopedia Judaica* 15:1238-39.

The Dual Transcending of Law / 111

> (5) God rewards obedience and punishes transgression. (6) The law provides for means of atonement, and atonement results in (7) maintenance or re-establishment of the covenantal relationship. (8) All those who are maintained in the covenant by obedience, atonement and God's mercy belong to the group which will be saved. An important interpretation of the first and last points is that election and ultimately salvation are considered to be by God's mercy rather than human achievement.[14]

Sanders sees an emphasis upon the prior grace of God as central to the sense of law. "Often the Rabbis speak of God as King, not an oriental despot who rules without consent, but one who solicits assent by first saving and protecting the people, and who only then gives commandments."[15] God is the gracious Other who guides those standing in the covenantal relationship. Law has, by no means, exhausted its role with the birth of faith or the awareness of covenant. This is reiterated in the refrain found at the end of each section of the "Aboth: Sayings of the Fathers" in the Hebrew *Daily Prayer Book*:

> Rabbi Chanaya, the son of Akashya, said, The Holy One, blessed be he, was pleased to make Israel worthy; wherefore he gave them a copious Torah and many commandments; as it is said, It pleased the Lord, for his righteousness' sake, to magnify the Torah and make it honourable.

This is expanded in a footnote:

> *copious Torah and many commandments.* "These words may be a polemic against the subversive doctrine of Paul concerning the Torah. Here it is asserted that there is no greater proof of God's love to Israel than the multitude of commandments He has given Israel. They were the gracious gift of God, designed to train Israel in moral holiness, and make them all the more worthy in the eyes of the Holy One, blessed be He." (I. Epstein)[16]

George Mendenhall draws attention to this same alternative sense of law, although, perhaps as a Lutheran, he avoids the term. He contrasts "a power structure and a community."[17] Not synonymous with Turner's communitas, community here implies a society

---

14 E. P. Sanders, *Paul and Palestinian Judaism* (Philadelphia: Fortress Press, 1977), p. 422.
15 Ibid., p. 236.
16 *The Authorized Daily Prayer Book*, with commentary and notes by Dr. Joseph H. Hertz (New York: Bloch Publishing, 1960), p. 627.
17 George E. Mendenhall, "The Conflict Between Values Systems and Social Control," in Hans Goedicke and J. J. Roberts (eds.), *Unity and Diversity* (Baltimore: Johns Hopkins University Press, 1975), p. 173.

organized in terms of free allegiance to a value system founded on some transcendent reality, rather than a structure sustained through the exercise of power. Mendenhall distinguishes between covenant and law, covenant being the structuring of a meaning system that lies at the basis of community and even creates community where none has existed, in contrast to law that presupposes some social order and is an instrument for maintaining that order. Covenant rests upon gratitude, law upon social fear; covenant is oriented towards the future and creativity, law towards the past and punishment. Whether or not these discussions offer a complete and accurate picture of Paul, Luther, or Judaism, they emphasize the need to recognize a second basic function of law as guidance.

As implied in the previous chapter, Peter Berger adopts the term "nomos" for law in its ordering function, be that reflected in the communal ordering exercised by social structure or in the meanings and values sustained by myth, rituals, and religion. "The socially constructed world," he writes, "is, above all, an ordering of experience. A meaningful order, or nomos, is imposed upon the discrete experiences and meanings of individuals."[18] I have already used the term implicitly with this connotation. Let me now employ it explicitly—though not exclusively in a sociological context—to draw a contrast between *the moral and the nomic functions of law*. Law in its moral function is an imperative. "Thou shalt... Thou shalt not...." In its nomic function, it is an indicative. "Herein is truth, beauty, and goodness." It is this second sense of law (torah, nomos, guidance, order, teaching) that I have in mind when I speak of a second law-gospel tension ultimately leading to the transnomic. Law, in both its moral and nomic functions, can exercise bondage to the point of tyranny.

Nomos appears in the structure and the shared meanings of a society. But what is taken to be the obvious, hence unchallenged, validity of the shared world-taken-for-granted constitutes a limitation on the possibilities for conception and understanding. Some things are literally inconceivable for the participants in a shared nomos. Marxist criticism has drawn attention to this bondage in the form of class bias. At the same time as we are provided a point from which to view reality, the very social perspective from which we look out upon the world means that we are left with the limitations of that viewpoint, limitations all the more dangerous when unrecognized. The order by which we make sense of experience to a large extent confines us to

18 Berger, *Sacred Canopy*, p. 19.

The Dual Transcending of Law / 113

the experience that the order acknowledges. Assuredly, such bondage becomes more obvious in the mechanisms used by those who support the nomos, not only to socialize the young into the world-taken-for-granted but also to suppress the efforts of all those within the society who would challenge the accepted understandings. For the former, there are the many styles of legitimation, including the appeal to divine origins. For the latter, extreme measures, including the death sentence or banishment from the society, may be employed, all deemed to be correct and acceptable according to the shared meanings of the community. As we saw in the previous chapter, such control can also be exercised through the domestication of the liminal, the parabolic, or the subversive elements of society. Turner noted, for example, that in traditional societies the very liminal moments occurring in rites of passage become a means by which "traditional authority nips radical deviation in the bud."[19] Rites of ritual mocking, the Feast of Fools—or even the remnant still found in the celebration of Mardi Gras—are moments of boisterous rebellion which, however, are structurally organized to sustain the nomos. Thus occasions of protest are made to serve the preservation of bondage. The relative decline of pilgrimage in Christian culture, we saw, is associated with the inability of the established ecclesial structures to control the impact of pilgrimage, to limit its liminal, socially critical, function. In short, to live in a society, to share its nomos, its world-taken-for-granted, or, as Berger puts it, to remain a participant in the ongoing conversation of a people, is nevertheless to be enmeshed in their understanding with one's capacity to conceptualize in new ways limited by the power of this nomos.

An examination of therapeutic experience reveals the same phenomenon; the existence of structure, order, nomos, though essential for human functioning, still limits and in some cases leads to a psychopathology. It is difficult to make a sharp separation between the operation of moral and nomic bondage in this instance. Yet, I suggest, one can discern more than enslavement to the moral imperative in patients. Some operate under the tyranny of a framework for ordering life. In *The Structure of Magic*, Bandler and Grinder state that patients' problems derive from this framework which either distorts their experience or unnecessarily limits their options in responding to life. The patients' world-taken-for-granted, not the world in itself, is the problem. "The limitations which they experience are, typically, in their *representation* of the world and not in the world

19 Turner and Turner, *Image and Pilgrimage*, p. 3.

itself."[20] In the first depth analytical discussions of Freud and Adler, neurotic bondage was also associated with their clients' frame of reference, their interpretation of reality. Both men associated this with potent memories which had played a key role in developing a sense of identity. Thus, in Freud's famous phrase, his patients "suffered from reminiscences." Even in many of the optimistic, humanistic therapies, one still finds recognition of an order which, if maladaptive, can exercise a pathogenic tyranny. Transactional analysts speak of our living in "scripts" that set the structure, expectations, and limitations for life, patterns thought again to be significantly shaped in early life. The task of psychotherapy is to break the power of such bondage, to end the sense of impotence before fate, and to create in the patients a freedom to take charge of life, to rewrite their script.

Within the religious context, the nomos found in the myths, rituals, ecclesial structures, and theologies of a faith community, whatever their virtue, can also constitute imprisonment. We see this most starkly in the suppression of the infidel by the true believer. The Spanish Inquisition, the Puritan witch hunts, and the deadly courts of the Ayatollah Khomeini are obvious examples of such tyranny. Today's attacks upon those deemed to foster heretical beliefs in such things as evolution or welfare, or to follow lifestyles beyond the pale, such as the homosexual, while less crudely violent, represent the same tyrannical imposition of the one, true nomos. But nomic oppression is not confined to inquisitors and leaders of the moral majority, to those who would exercise external and, sometimes, brutal force to ensure compliance. Arrogant dogmatism may be merely the defensive expression of those who cannot tolerate exposure to alternative visions. Indeed, few men and women of faith avoid all bondage, especially to their own convictions and symbols. Under the impact of feminist criticism, many Christians and Jews are becoming aware that the assurance they have found in the image of God as their Father has limited their capacity to appreciate fully the reality of women. So great is this bondage that some, like Mary Daly in *Beyond God the Father*, have argued that women can find no freedom or fulfillment in the biblical nomos; they must break free from Yahweh and Son. Nomos, as theologies, can restrict the human spirit. Tragically, Christians at times have preached freedom from the law, conceived of in its moral function, in a way that imposes their theology as a new tyranny, this time as a nomic bondage. As the

---

20 Bandler and Grinder, *Structure of Magic*, vol. 2, p. 3.

moral law can be experienced in both the positive and negative conscience, so nomic bondage may be exercised either as an imposed order, the dogmatism of another, or as freely and unambiguously self-imposed bondage, the tyranny of our own fundamentalism.

We have seen that the transmoral conscience does not mean the abolition of the moral imperative. Similarly, the transnomic, which I now seek to elucidate, does not entail the destruction of nomos, for this would mean the end of all order and structure. Peter Berger forcefully maintains in *The Sacred Copy* that destroying nomos can give birth to chaos. He cites the dramatic example of the murder of Atahualpa, the Inca, by the Spaniards as a "world-shattering catastrophe" from which Inca civilization never really recovered. The symbolic link with the gods and thus, with order, was simply and unceremoniously swept away. Likewise, Turner places strong emphasis upon the power and importance of the liminal, challenging dimension of social experience, but still he asserts that there is no guarantee such disruption will necessarily result in something positive. The abolition of the nomos may lead only to the chaos of "a Hobbesian war of all against all, or an existentialist anarchy of individuals."[21] Berger has elsewhere described nomos "as a shield against terror."[22] Mankind cannot live without order and meaning; hence the most important function of society is nomization. Concerning the effect upon individuals, Bruno Bettelheim describes in *The Informed Heart* the traumatic impact achieved in the concentration camps by the deliberate disruption of all ordered expectations for the inmates where rebellion was periodically rewarded and obedience punished. All capacity to interpret the situation correctly, all attempts to develop a framework, were so shattered that the prisoners disintegrated into senseless zombies. In his extensive discussion of identity, Erikson articulates the severe trauma that can follow from the loss of our personal, psychological nomos. It seems fair to say that men and women cannot exist—or, at any rate, cannot exist for long or very well—without some nomos. Society cannot function without some elements of order, some definition of roles, relationships, and expectations. To quote Turner again, we must oppose the "bureaucratic *ubermensch* who would array the whole world of lesser men in terms of hierarchy and regimentation," but equally we must resist "the puritanical levelers who would abolish all idiosyncratic differences

---

21 Turner, *Dramas, Fields, and Metaphors*, p. 285.
22 Berger, *Sacred Canopy*, p. 22.

between man and man."[23] Therapy entails not only overcoming bondage to pathological memories, distorted scripts, and twisted identities, but also the creation of salutary, healing self- and world-images. In Winnicott's discussion, one must first establish a secure base, a nomos, before the final act of therapy—which is play—can begin. In theological terms, not only is there the necessity for law in its moral function, but there remains a place for its nomic activity as well, that which Tillich calls the inevitable "Catholic substance." There is no way to think about God without some framework for our thought. The issue is whether the frameworks within which we think—as individuals, as citizens, as people of faith—the frameworks of our psyches, our societies, and our theologies, are creative or destructive, healing or pathogenic. The nomos is necessary. The crux of the matter, however, lies not only in its character but also in our relationship to it. Even a healing structure can become destructive if we do not possess some capacity to transcend it, to escape its bondage.

The transnomic can be both compared and contrasted with Tillich's transmoral. In the case of the transmoral conscience one maintains the sense of moral urgency, the reality of ethical claims, but no longer experiences these as a call to achievement, to self-justification, to active righteousness. The moral law, while a preparation for the gospel, ceases to have a proper place within the self as redeemed. Law (as a moral imperative) and gospel are mutually exclusive. In transnomic experience, one again moves beyond nomos, outside the confines of structure and order without, however, denying the continuing validity of the nomos, even for those who know the transnomic experience. Here we have a higher order of experience which does not spell the abolition of the lower. Nomos is taken up into the transnomic in a sense that the moral is not taken up into the transmoral.

How does the nomic relate to the transnomic? Victor Turner identifies for us the transnomic's threefold function. The first two define the function of the transnomic (the liminal) in terms of its service to the nomic (to structure). In the third instance the transnomic is defined in terms of its innate worth, quite apart from the nomic.

In the first place, the liminal provides a means for social criticism, an examination of the basic assumptions and ultimate understandings of a tribe or culture. Liminality "as a time and place of withdrawal from the normal modes of social action . . . can be seen as potentially

---

23 Turner, *Dramas, Fields, and Metaphors*, p. 268.

a period of scrutinization of the central values and axioms of the culture in which it occurs."[24] Standing apart from the nomos, one is given another viewpoint, allowing in turn a new evaluation of society's perspective. By the same process, liminality offers a second service to the nomos, namely, a creative function. It is also potentiality; it means thinking the unthinkable, conceiving that which is nomically inconceivable or, at best, nonsense. The great ecstatic thinkers—for Turner, the poets, prophets, and seers—are in fact the true creators of worlds. They provide "the conditions for the production of root metaphors, conceptual archetypes, paradigms, models for, and the rest."[25] Thus, the transnomic, in this parabolic sense, is the moment in which the individual or group transcends society, making possible its criticism and higher, more creative expressions of the nomos. Indeed, Turner sees an inevitable dialectic between the nomic and the transnomic, a dialectic that energizes and drives the development of societies and human conceptualizations. "Man is both a structural and an anti-structural entity, who *grows* through anti-structure and *conserves* through structure."[26] We make progress (or at least develop) in the critical moment of the transnomic but inevitably conserve our insights in a new articulation of our reformed nomos.

I have suggested in an earlier chapter that the full use of story both in its nomic and transnomic aspects, in its affirming and disruptive functions, has not been as widely developed and appreciated in therapy as would seem to be desirable. Nevertheless, one does find a sense of this twofold function of the transnomic in the service of the nomic. The transnomic as fantasy, as a creative moment, has been highlighted by several of the authors studied. James Hillman, we have seen, describes fantasy as a "creative activity" which frees a person to try on new stories, this nomos and that one, a process of nomic refinement.[27] Augusta Jellinek discusses the production of new images and symbols through fantasy which the patients are told not to interpret (i.e., not to press back into the old nomos?), but to use purposefully to influence their behaviour and attitudes in the creation of an improved, expanded self- and world-image. Such is my interpretation of her attitude to fantasy. In the Gouldings' work one finds both the critical and creative functions of the transnomic.

24　Turner, *The Ritual Process*, p. 167.
25　Turner, *Dramas, Fields, and Metaphors*, p. 50.
26　Ibid., p. 298 (his emphasis).
27　Hillman, *Loose Ends*, p. 2.

> In redecision therapy the client experiences the child part of self, enjoys his childlike qualities, and creates fantasy scenes in which he can safely give up restricting decisions he made in childhood.... This time [he] *does the scene the way he wants to do it.*[28]

The transnomic, however, is not limited simply to service of the nomic. Whereas Berger suggested that to leave the nomos was primarily to run the danger of anomy and chaos, we saw that Turner maintained another possibility, namely, communitas. Communitas is a state of immediate and intense human community, a sense of being present one to another, that transcends the definitions of social structures and the tendency to reduce the other to an occupant of a role. Although it is impossible to remain constantly in that state, communitas, the transnomic moment, is an experience of a higher, deeper, more fully human sense of being. It is truly an ecstatic state, one in which we step out of the nomos into creative freedom. Given the psychotherapeutic focus upon healing nomic distortion, the creation of a more functional sense of identity, it is not surprising that the transnomic is articulated in terms more of its service to the nomic than of its own intrinsic worth. Nevertheless, Winnicott's claim that healing and growth are fostered most effectively when the patient and therapist can play together would seem expressive of the thought that our humanness is enriched as we are transnomic. We are most truly human when we play. The recent call in several forms of psychotherapy for a recovery of the childlike and playful dimensions of personality sounds a similar note. Play and fantasy may indeed be the therapeutic parallel to Turner's communitas.

Let me suggest one further relationship between the nomic and the transnomic, one not developed by Turner, namely, the nomic in service of the transnomic. If one thinks again of the contrast between law and covenant, between community and power structure, it becomes immediately apparent that a nomos can either enhance or lessen the chances of experiencing communitas. In like manner, our sense of identity, our representation of the world, can either increase or decrease the potential for freedom, fantasy, and playfulness. This is surely part of what is involved in the recognition that innately our social structures and our stories can be healing or destructive, not only in terms of the nomic but also in terms of our capacity for the transnomic.

Has this discussion of the transnomic any relationship to the religious and theological scene? In my earlier work, when analyzing

---

28 Mary and Robert Goulding, *Changing Lives*, p. 9 (their emphasis).

The Dual Transcending of Law / 119

Luther's and Calvin's third use of the law, what I now call the law's "nomic" function, I pointed out the distinctly different emphasis of the two reformers. Luther tended to think of the life of faith in almost anti-nomian terms. He could discuss the Ten Commandments as the expression of God's will for mankind, but his focus was upon the spontaneous, immediate, joyous response of the faithful, to the point of being highly contextual. It was transnomic in a parabolic sense, rejecting the rigidity of any code or structure. So a contemporary interpreter of Luther writes, "There is no law for the conduct of life, no law which can be learned as a future requirement or as a standard of saintliness, whereby the ethical life of 'the converted' can be guided into the right furrow."[29] Meanwhile, Calvin's emphasis upon Christian obedience and the glory of God tended, in practice, to give a more rigid, almost legalistic tone to his discussion of the life of faith. In fact, his Genevan church exercised a very rigorous discipline upon the citizenry. It can be argued that each of the reformers was guarding a different aspect of the transnomic experience which the other was in danger of neglecting. In their emphasis, however, each ran the risk of losing something of the dynamic whole. So Luther stressed the transnomic as freedom from nomic bondage, while Calvin emphasized that even in the transnomic moment we can only understand ourselves in relation to the structure which brought us to that experience. Brunner alludes to this complementary character of the two theologians:

> It is good, and willed by God, that Zwingli and Calvin stand alongside of Luther, in order that Luther's doctrine of the liberty of the children of God should not be degraded into the "freedom of the flesh." And it is also good that Luther stands alongside of Calvin and Zwingli, in order that the obedience of faith and the emphasis on the instruction of the law should not once more slip into legalism.[30]

One senses similar tension when Sam Keen in *To a Dancing God* warns that "spontaneity has replaced storytelling as the mode of authentic life."[31] Spontaneity here is what Turner meant by the "liminality of solitude." It is normlessness, anomy, a position that rejects the need for a structure in life, for the living identity that is one's story. "Genuine spontaneity," Keen claims, "is possible only to the person who has accepted the limits imposed upon him by his past

---

29 G. Wingren, *Luther on Vocation* (Philadelphia: Muhlenberg Press, 1957), p. 202.
30 Brunner, *Divine Imperative*, p. 81.
31 Sam Keen, *To a Dancing God* (New York: Harper & Row, 1970), p. 97.

experience and who is animated by some meaning he seeks to realize in his future."[32] In this instance it savours the transnomic moment, one that passes beyond story, nomos, and any bondage, but does so without denying the validity of the earlier moment. Robert McAfee Brown's discussion of the creative appropriation of one's past would likewise suggest the transnomic in the service of the nomic, emphasizing freedom to rethink and redefine one's past in order to discern more responsibly one's values and commitment in the present.[33]. Paul Tillich sets forth these issues most systematically in his contrast between the "Protestant principle" and "Catholic substance."[34] The former is parabolic, anti-nomic. Affirming that truth finally is found in God alone, it rejects as demonic all human claims—intellectual, moral, and religious—to infallibility. The latter is mythic or nomic. It is the inevitably concrete expression of our spiritual experience and understanding. The dynamic relationship between the two in the articulation of faith clearly is very reminiscent of Turner's dialectic between structure and anti-structure in the evolution of society and culture. Finally, Crossan asserts that only when "the deep structure of our accepted world [our nomos]" is shattered do we become "vulnerable to God" and truly open to experience transcendence—which is a theological claim for the intrinsic value of the transnomic moment of and for itself.[35]

How, then, does one envisage law as nomos in this context? If we are looking for an image, I suggest that we might conceive of law not so much as a beacon light that marks our goal, capturing or defining the end towards which we move. Rather, it is a beacon that guides but points beyond itself. Perhaps it is a note which, by sounding, helps our quest but might, on occasion, even sound from behind us. Let us think of the beacon, the note, that helps us move in the direction where communitas is more likely, where the free, childlike, playful self more easily can come to life, where we encounter that which is truly transcendent or divine. Such a law remains relevant in the life of any individual or community, whether or not it is expressed in traditionally religious terms. As admonished in the Bible, we must test the spirits, we must test the validity of what we believe to be communitas, the freedom of the children of God. Our theologies help with the testing. However, the ultimate reality is not our nomos, but

32 Ibid., p. 98.
33 Robert McAfee Brown, *Is Faith Obsolete?* (Philadelphia: Westminster Press, 1974), pp. 41-65.
34 Tillich, *Systematic Theology*, vol. 3, p. 245.
35 Crossan, *The Dark Interval*, p. 122.

freedom and grace. Law, as nomos, cannot define our goal in advance, although it remains relevant in advance of all ventures toward that goal. Consequently, to speak of the transnomic is not only to allude to a moment of higher, richer, human experience, but also to invoke an attitude toward the inevitable structures and orders of life.

The religious perspective also casts light upon the issue of law, the transmoral and the transnomic in terms of mankind's twofold quest for security. In *What is Man?* Wolfhart Pannenberg remarks, "Where a person can control things, then everyone will probably prefer to make himself safe instead of entering into a relationship of trust, which is always risky. Therefore a person will probably always strive, where possible, to replace trust with control."[36] This is true for our technological control of nature and, even more significantly, for our relationship with God. "Man's religions are thoroughly characterized by the striving for security and by the effort to get hold of the deity and his saving power."[37] Pannenberg observes that when we seek to develop such means of control, such power within ourselves, we become enslaved by our own tools and inventions. We must meet the demands of the instrumentalities of our own security. We end in bondage to that which was supposed to make us secure. As set forth in *Ethical Confrontation in Counseling*, this phenomenon has been developed in theology, primarily in relation to morality. Law becomes the definition of those things that guarantee our right to be, that secure our justification, but in that very event law becomes a tyranny. The portrait of moral goodness becomes an imperative. We begin by demanding the right to save ourselves and end with the impossible requirement that we do just that. The experience of a transmoral basis for our existence opens the way beyond such bondage. In a parallel sense, I am arguing that even those who are convinced of the free grace of God, despite their moral failure, may seek to make this new conviction free from all doubt and imprecision by demanding the security of an absolute knowledge of God. In that very moment, they become the possession of their understanding. They are in bondage to their own, always finite, knowledge. As we must learn to trust God in the context of our moral shortcomings, so we must trust him in the context of our finite understanding. We are secure no more in the perfection of our theology than in the holiness of our conduct. Faith, in relationship to the transmoral, is not the

36 Wolfhart Pannenberg, *What is Man?* (Philadelphia: Fortress Press, 1970), p. 34.
37 Ibid., p. 35.

assurance of our moral virtue but the "encounter with a morally alluring graciousness, with that which theists have called the holy and loving God."[38] Faith, in relationship to the transnomic, is the recognition that we do not possess infallible information but that we are called to venture—even dance—with a trusted friend.

When Moses encountered God in the burning bush, he asked to be given the divine name. To learn the name of God was to possess an understanding, to gain power. In our terms, Moses wanted nomic security. He was given only the enigmatic title which scholars have translated in so many ways, or have left as untranslatable. "I am what I am"; "I shall be what I shall be"; "I cause to be what comes to be"; or simply, "I am." "Tell them," God commanded, "that I am sent you." In effect, he was denied nomic security and called upon to trust. "I will be, or am, with you" was all Moses was assured (Exodus 3). Similarly, it is arguable that in the farewell discourses of the Fourth Gospel, when Jesus says to the disciples, "It is for your good that I am leaving you. If I do not go, your Advocate will not come, whereas if I go I will send him to you" (John 16:7), we have a reference to the transnomic. It was necessary that the Incarnate Lord, the particular, historical expression that Cobb and Driver call the "Christ past," be replaced by a more dynamic, less fixed reality, but nonetheless one that bears witness to and is in keeping with the spirit of the Incarnate. Such a reading becomes the more appealing if Gordon Kaufman is correct in suggesting that the Advocate, "Paraclete," is better translated as "Companion"—One who travels with us rather than fixedly defines the end.[39] As we shall see in the next chapter, both Driver and Cobb struggle to articulate what can be called a transnomic Christology, one born from the New Testament understanding, yet which transcends the inevitable limitations of any particular expression of the truth. Their reference to the dynamic Christ of the present-future has much the flavour of Kaufman's "Companion." Finally, Jurgen Moltmann distinguishes between religions of promise and religions of epiphany. The latter claim to possess the sure knowledge of God from the moment of revelation, "an epiphany of the divine, eternal, *immutable*,"[40] granting nomic security. The former call for trust in the promises of God and for hope

38 Hoffman, *Ethical Confrontation in Counseling*, p. 111.
39 Gordon Kaufman, *Systematic Theology: A Historicist Perspective* (New York: Charles Scribner's Sons, 1968), p. 228.
40 Jurgen Moltmann, *Theology of Hope* (New York: Harper & Row, 1967), p. 43 (my emphasis).

before an open future, for the adventure of faith which is transnomic. Indeed, Moltmann's whole theology of hope is a summons to the transnomic.

Let me turn briefly to the area of counseling. We are in a position to expand the discussion found in my earlier work. Applying the concept of the transnomic, I would emphasize some of its implications. Within the whole area that I previously called moral confrontation in counseling, one can distinguish the function of the transnomic in service of the nomic. The purely parabolic, as found in some therapies of the absurd, and more generally, the counter-mythic or counter-nomic in many kinds of counseling, offer counselees the opportunity to re-examine their own definitions of reality and value assumptions.

My other book presented the crucial role of internalized, moral perceptions, including their expression as unconscious, largely automatic, reactions. Where these are ethically sensitive and in harmony with the conscious desires and purposes of individuals, they can facilitate the whole process of moral decision, increasing the feeling of freedom and power in one's life. But such internalized laws may, in fact, be disruptive of spontaneous, free self-actualization. In the form of moral maladaptations, "the child's simplified framework for moral reference continues to function automatically in the adult, limiting the latter's ability to make adequate discriminations. Many forms of prejudice are examples of such ethical pathology."[41] More obviously, the consciously held ideals of men and women may be perceived by the counselor as inviting a morally inadequate lifestyle. "The child raised in a sociopathic subculture, in a Bonnie-and-Clyde type family, needs major moral reeducation."[42] Here we need not assume that we have moralistic bondage; such persons may be quite at peace. Whether moral maladaptations or sociopathic ideals, the counselor's task is not primarily one of assisting the other to experience the transmoral and thus gain freedom from bondage to achievement. Rather, it is to invite them to a transnomic posture that liberates them from bondage to their present understanding of goodness and truth and that frees them to rethink their frame of reference, their scripting.

Meanwhile, counselors must be sensitive to the transnomic in themselves. They must have a keen sense of the parabolic in relation to their own moral perceptions.

41 Hoffman, *Ethical Confrontation in Counseling*, pp. 81-82.
42 Ibid., p. 85.

> [T]he therapist must never forget that he can but witness to the ethical depths of life; he does not possess infallible moral insight. He is not God, however much the patient may tend to deify him in the transference relationship. Nevertheless, he can enrich the experience of therapeutic acceptance through the creative encounter with an ethical witness, the quality of his counsel being influenced by the quality of his own relation to moral values.[43]

Let me stress the sense of witness, of confession, in all this. The therapist's task is to offer not an infallible image or conception of truth, but rather an honest confession of ethical convictions which can sound as a reference point for counselees—if they so choose—as they struggle to define for themselves some proximate images of goodness and beauty to guide their own ventures in living. In the earlier work I remarked:

> Where justification and sanctification are meaningfully united in a "faith" experience, where [the therapist] has found the freedom and moral responsibility of the transmoral conscience, he will be more likely to convey this unity to the other. Knowing that his own right to be is founded not upon achievement but upon free grace, he will recognize that his relation to the client must also grant priority to love over achievement.[44]

I would but add, where his own understanding is infused with a sense of the transnomic as well, he will more likely assist the other to trust beyond the security of his own moral perceptions, to live with that faith which Tillich calls "the courage to be," the courage that can take into itself the ever present reality of "existential doubt."[45] Ultimately, the transnomic in itself, that sense of the free, spontaneous, loving and childlike existence which arises out of but transcends a host of nomic contexts, will become the goal of such counseling, that which Paul calls "the glorious liberty of the children of God" (Romans 8:21). Lest we become too rhapsodic, let us remember that these experiences of pure, transnomic freedom—for both counselor and counselee—will be but passing moments, this liberty often achieved only for limited aspects of their nomic bondage. Nonetheless, these will guide each in the struggle "to make and keep human life human."[46]

43 Ibid., pp. 107-08.
44 Ibid., p. 108.
45 Paul Tillich, *The Courage To Be* (New Haven: Yale University Press, 1952), passim.
46 Paul Lehmann, *Ethics in a Christian Context* (New York: Harper & Row, 1963), p. 101.

6

Towards a Transnomic Theology

In *Christ in a Changing World*, Tom F. Driver defines theology as what the Church *should* teach about God. It is not adequate merely to review past teachings.[1] Attention must also be paid to the present context and the moral consequences of doctrinal expression. Driver emphasizes the Church's responsibility for the ethical fallout of its teachings, in fostering, for example, racist and sexist attitudes. I want to adopt this image of theology, but also accentuate the need to accept responsibility for the attitudes engendered towards what we teach. Specifically, I suggest that what the Church teaches about God, the language it chooses and its forms of expression, should be such so as to invoke not only an awareness of its content, its nomos, but also a lively sense of the transnomic in relation to that content. The Church should speak of God in a way that, while bearing confessional witness to a truth, experience, and power, reminds others and itself that truth, healing, and power transcend the Church's articulation, that to be faithful means to resist the false security that comes with bondage to our theological systems. We need to be aware, as Peter Slater has stated, that "keeping faith with our predecessors means changing with the times as they did."[2]

1 Tom F. Driver, *Christ in a Changing World* (New York: Crossroad, 1981), p. 1.
2 Slater, *op. cit.*, pp. 2-3.

We need remember that even with a creatively functional theology, its very creativity depends, for full exercise, upon our being prepared to venture beyond the specifics of its content.

A transnomic theology will be transnomic in two ways. In the first place, it will be constantly self-critical or parabolic, reflecting what I have called the transnomic in service of the nomic. It will be marked by methodological doubt, the Protestant principle. Moreover, a fully transnomic theology must surely be one that, in its very expression, seeks to assist the believer in moving beyond the structures of theology to the transnomic experience, into freedom, communitas, play, and a sense of the transcendent. Such a theology will see its doctrines not as statements of ultimate truth, not as descriptions of the goal or point to be reached, but rather as starting points or guiding references that must themselves be transcended. William Temple approached this in his Gifford Lectures: "I do not believe in any creed, but I use certain creeds to express, to conserve, and to deepen my belief in God."[3]

Doctrines and creeds are defenses that define the outer limits of the realm of thought and experience which have served to guide the spiritual pilgrimage of a faith community. The early Christological creeds do not define the nature of the Christ; they express basic convictions which inspired and steered the religious quest, but whose full, positive content can never be captured by the creedal formulas. Nor must they be thought of as fortifications in which one dwells secure. Their protection is more like a beacon than a Maginot Line, and that beacon merely reflects the way we have found most fruitful for the Christian adventure *up to this time*.

At first glance, one may argue that there is not much that is new or startling in such demands. Yet how many times are our theologies offered in such a way that suggests "Use this in the pursuit of God but remember always that we have not captured God. This is not God."? Theologians have seldom claimed absolute truth for their systems and churches have seldom claimed perfection in every aspect of their teaching, but that is content. The mode of expression, on the other hand, all too often has suggested to the humble believer that it is close enough to be treated as such. It is not surprising that dogma is readily associated with dogmatism. In this light, I plead for a self-conscious attempt to express theology in a manner that evokes this twofold transnomic character, but one that must remain truly transnomic and not fall into anomic relativism. What would all this mean?

3 William Temple, *Nature, Man and God* (London: Macmillan, 1956), p. 322.

Let us begin by examining two relatively recent studies of Christology, Tom Driver's *Christ in a Changing World* and John Cobb's *Christ in a Pluralistic Age*. (Cobb's is the older work by half a dozen years, but I shall look first at Driver.) Both seem to reflect an awareness of the need for a transnomic theology, though, of course, they do not employ my terminology; both struggle to escape a destructive bondage to past formulations concerning the person of Jesus and his meaning for our time, bondage with a potential for tyranny at the very core of Christian faith. They feel the chafing of this bondage in different ways. Cobb's emphasis is upon the interface with other world religions, Driver's upon the ethical inadequacies of past Christologies. Each offers, I believe, a theology alive to the constant need for the Protestant principle, for the transnomic in service of the nomic, even though each assumes a different shape. Neither, I would judge, yet succeeds in evoking the second sense of a transnomic theology, the witness that invites an adventure of faith that goes beyond all structure, definition, or nomos.

Driver's Parabolic Theology

Driver maintains that theology is what the Church should teach about God. In this context, Christology becomes an examination of what the Church should teach about Christ. A basic principle, therefore, of his methodology is that "the proposed christology shall be subjected, while it is formulated, to ethical judgment."[4] In taking this stand Driver is partly reacting against the privatization of religion that transforms Christianity primarily into a relationship between the individual soul and God. Found in much popular Jesus-piety, it turns away from the social and ethical implications of faith. Driver is even more concerned about the tragic social fallout of much past Christological teaching. Institutions and beliefs that do not lead to greater freedom and the enrichment of human life cannot be regarded as the truth. Driver expresses his concern "that the worship of God in Christ not divide Christian from Jew, man from woman, clergy from laity, white from black or rich from poor."[5] The sad reality of Christianity, however, is that, in its allegiance to Jesus, in the proclamation of Christ as Lord, it has been in constant danger of fostering what Dorothee Soelle calls "christofascism," the arrogant, totalitarian, imperialistic attitude which assaults the humanity of

---

4 Driver, *Christ in a Changing World*, p. 21.
5 Ibid., p. 5.

many. Christianity, Driver finds, has been guilty of encouraging a latent doctrine of non-persons in association with its high Christology. The universal and exclusive claims that Christians made for Christ within the confines of the New Testament resulted, even then, in anti-Semitism, in declaring the non-person status of the Jews. Today we see it also in racism and sexism. Since Jesus was a white male, non-males and non-whites were threatened with being regarded as non-persons. Assuredly, the roots of both sexism and racism are much broader than Christology, but Driver feels that traditional Christological focus has supported such attitudes. If we would take seriously the ethical challenges before us, a major rethinking of our Christology is required. "The question is how to be a Christian without being paternalistic of those who are not."[6]

In the terms of our discussion, Driver sees the problem as lying in the nomic rigidity of traditional orthodoxy which inhibits a creative and open response to the moral dilemmas of our time. "Insofar as Jesus is thought to be archetype, norm, or model of human being, or insofar as he is held to be the center of all value, Christian ethics is crippled. The model is insufficient."[7] He argues that most New Testament writers did not think of Jesus as offering a life-model for this world. In the atmosphere of the profoundly eschatological expectations of that early community, they looked for this world to pass away. The problems of ethical life, of moral and just social structures, were consequently of limited interest. But Christian orthodoxy, sadly enough, developed a form that amounted to an idolatry of the past, which could not help but subjugate the freedom and openness of the present and future to its rigid structures.

Driver's emphasis upon the ethical implications of faith requires, as he sees it, a concentration upon the future or the present-future, the time of moral decision and action, rather than upon the past. An excessive concern with what our ancestors would have done or what has been stated in the doctrinal systems of the Church, rather than with the moral implications of our present experience, is in fact to worship our ancestors and their doctrines instead of the God of the present and future who is able to change the very context within which we must make our choices. "The main purpose of the church is not to remember Jesus. Its main purpose, surely, is to participate now, in the present-future time, in the redemption of the world."[8]

6   Ibid., p. 58.
7   Ibid., p. 55.
8   Ibid., p. 11.

Driver's Christology calls for a subordination of the first-century historical Jesus and the New Testament record to the twentieth-century actions of God in our present-future. Our discernment of this God is normative for religion, in contrast to the traditional, theological methods that have begun with the past, with the "eternal truths," and have seen their assignment only as the restatement of the perennial nomos. No longer can we accept a fixed domain of doctrine that sets limits to what can and should be said now regarding nature, mankind, God, and the future. If we are to be capable of responding adequately to the moral challenges of our time, we must be open to encounter that which is truly new, which transcends past experience. Martin Luther and the Protestant Reformation represented a rebellion against the nomic tyranny of ecclesiastical structures and defined faith, a rebellion expressed by Luther in his appeal to the Bible as the Word of God. Yet this, in turn, has taken form in new idolatry of the past. Scripture has become the divine nomos, the new rigidity. However effective the Bible may have been in expressing the truth in its time, it cannot provide "the adaptive and creative strategies which are necessary now for the survival of humanity on earth."[9] It is not that the Bible has no place within the Christian tradition, but idolatry of the Bible as the received Word of God builds a rigidity that stifles the creative response of spirit. Doctrinally, this emerges in two forms, spatially, so to speak, in Christ as the centre of life, and temporally, in that which was in Christ being once for all.

Driver takes seriously the intense, eschatological expectations of the first century. When disillusioned because Jesus, who was to lead into a new and open future, did not return to establish the new order, the Kingdom of God, Christian theology underwent a paradigm shift in its understanding. "The shift was to move the Messiah from the *lead edge* of history to its *center*. At the lead edge, he was the herald of the future. At the center he became the embodiment of a humanity already made perfect in God."[10] Driver sees this as understandable, given the deep hold Jesus had upon the Christian imagination and the importance he held in the self-image of Christians as over against the Jewish community. It would have been humiliating to admit that the messianic hopes had been wrong. Moreover, the new faith was being articulated at a time when the former centre of the world—Rome—was collapsing. So it was that the Christian community reinterpreted Christ as the centre of history, the norm of human life.

---

9 Ibid., p. 83.
10 Ibid., p. 40. Cf. p. 18.

(Unfortunately, this defined the Jews as being in error, from which the idea of Jews as non-persons germinated, which is a continuing blight on Christianity.) Most Christians cannot conceive of Christ other than at the centre. In a similar manner, the Christians came to speak of Jesus as God's once only, good-for-all-time action. Christ made the "once, perfect . . . sacrifice for the sins of the whole world."[11] This image, in effect, imprisons God within the likeness of Jesus. Why, Driver asks, must we assume that the "infinite commitment of God to human finitude" in Jesus (which, for him, is the meaning of the Incarnation) indicates something done but once and once only for all time?[12] Why is the divine commitment to this world and to history confined to that moment? The theology of hope is criticized by Driver precisely because it does not escape from the past. In its promise-hope image, it leaves the future too dependent upon the past and fails to take seriously the present-future dimension and thus the role of experience. Essentially, he finds all contemporary Christologies, including that of John Cobb, binding their understanding too closely to the historical Jesus. This is to focus upon a fixed and really dead Jesus of history, a Christ past, and to miss the actually living and changing Christ future.

In what sense can we properly describe this as a transnomic Christology? At the first level, we can at least say that it is anti-nomic in its denial of definition by the past, in its rejection of any kind of past-given order or structure, which limits present conceptualization. Nomic Christology is not able to respond adequately to the new. "It is a fundamental error, and a costly one, for theology to seek the truth of God and the truth of Christianity exclusively in Christ past, to the neglect of the truth involved in Christians' encounters with their changing environments."[13] Christian ethics must be oriented towards the present-future, the "more" at the edge of vision. No past structure is adequate to the changing realities of present experience, nor to the open possibilities of the future. The very demand for a fully moral response leads Driver to seek an anti-nomic or anti-structural rejection of definition by the past. This character is expressed, not only negatively in the parabolic dimension of Driver's Christology, not simply in his rejection of Christ past as inadequate, but also positively in his call for a new Christian model. Christianity must undergo a paradigm shift, even as it did in the first century, but the former must

11 Ibid., p. 25.
12 Ibid., p. 60.
13 Ibid., p. 47.

reverse the error of the latter. In phrases reminiscent of the theology of hope, he speaks of understanding God in terms of future and of advent, rather than in categories of the past and of epiphany. One needs to think of infinity not as some state or substance, but as a dynamic reaching beyond itself towards some future completion. Christ should be considered not so much as the Incarnate Lord of the past as the coming reality of the future. "[T]he one Christians should expect, is not Jesus of Nazareth, not Christ past but Christ future."[14] It is the definition of Christ future in terms of Christ past, in terms of the biblical promises, that locks the theology of hope into a hope-memory context which fails to come to grips with the present and which subsequently bars the way to a new future. Driver sees theologies of hope, by our terms, still too nomic.

The paradigm shift that Driver is seeking requires theology to take pluralism and relativity seriously, seeing them not as problems but as part of the dynamic and creative possibilities of life. "Instead of assuming that unity is prior to diversity, relativity understands unity as a creative process engendered by the prior existence of plurality."[15] Even modern process theology he finds wanting when it posits a prior, primordial nature in God. Relativity need not mean relativism, especially a moral relativism which says anything goes. Rather it considers that all things are "relative to" other realities. Thus Christianity must view itself as a religion, relative to other religions, and to the times in which it has had to express itself. Christian ethics must be relative to the circumstances wherein the Christian is called to act. We must learn to think of both God and Christ as relative. The concept of Christ no longer can be defined solely, perhaps even primarily, by Christ past, the Jesus of history. Rather Driver suggests, "We need to understand that 'Christ' is the changing pattern of our relation to a living God. The Christological task is to discern the features of this pattern in present-future time, and the only way to do this is to take with radical seriousness our ethical expectations."[16] Indeed, Driver can be open to the thought of a "plurality of Christs." Similarly, if we define God as fixed, the same yesterday, today and into the future, then we cannot really have an open and responsive ethic. It seems clear that Driver is not simply alluding to our conception of God. Granted, if God is relative to mankind, if God truly interacts with us, then God changes and so, too, the implications of his call for human

14 Ibid., p. 45.
15 Ibid., p. 67.
16 Ibid., p. 75.

action. We must, therefore, transcend the nomos of the past, recognizing that any order is relative and changing. With no fixed order, past, present or future, we have an open, dynamic, flowing conception of God and of Christ. Driver interprets the Holy Spirit as "that meaningful power of God's life which is infinite and which *resists figuration.*"[17] It is the ineffable component of divinity. His doctrine of the Trinity incorporates a dynamic within God, resistant to nomic definition. This maintains within the Christian image the open, antistructural understanding of God which is essential for a morally responsible theology.

Thus far, we might say that Driver's Christology is anti-nomic, but is it transnomic? I find his account reflecting many of the transnomic characteristics in our psychological and sociological discussions. These may be expressed indirectly through language that is either counter-structural or purely parabolic. Moreover, they evoke a sense of freedom, increased creativity and the experience of heightened community. One finds the counter-mythic in Driver's search for a new christic image which can aid imagination to think and feel its way past the destructive dualisms that have plagued the Christian interpretation of sexuality. What we need is a new conception of the Christ, enabling us to discard the distorting limitations of past interpretations, to scrap the imperialistic myth of "the all-male male."[18] So Driver ends his discussion of woman, man, and Christ: "We look for a Christ to help us emerge, and we wonder where she is. It is as if we had lost way back in infancy our sister Christ, or as if we are awaiting her to be born."[19] At other times, his language sounds simply parabolic. "Some kind of repudiation is necessary in order to break the power not of Christ but of the christocentric paradigm we have inherited."[20] Driver even finds the central motif of the resurrection parabolic, an image whose very character breaks open the structures of life. "To deny the finality of death is also to deny the authority assumed to belong to government, law, tradition, religious observance, natural causation, and anything else that may be regarded as 'the way it is.' If death is not final, all the cards in the deck may be wild."[21]

More positively, the Christology he seeks to expound could bring us a creative capacity with which to respond to ethical challenges

17   Ibid., p. 108 (my emphasis).
18   Ibid., p. 143.
19   Ibid., p. 145.
20   Ibid., p. 45.
21   Ibid., p. 18.

of life. We need have the courage to make the true leap of faith, the honesty not to slip back into the easy clichés of piety, but to break out of these by a venture of the imagination, knowing that "the result can be shocking."[22] This courageous imagination, this freedom to think the new thought, is a requisite, if we would truly appropriate for our time the reality of God in Christ. Our Christology must foster not merely an obedient remembrance of the past but an empowering leap into the future. To stand in relationship to the reality which Christ symbolizes means to stand in freedom from Christ. Driver puts it dramatically:

> To value that finite life, to prize, hold dear, and rejoice in that God-obsessed, itinerant, ascetic, male, wonder-working, Jewish, apocalyptic, crucified, resurrected, big-hearted, deep-suffering wayfarer born in an age remote from us now is to break free of trying to model ourselves upon him.[23]

Finally, it is particularly interesting to note Driver's association of christic experience with *communitas*, a term he adopts from Turner. For him the true experience of Christ is an experience of community that transcends the limitations and definitions of social structure, role, and rank. In language, in many ways reflective of Turner, he remarks that the Christian gospel is not—in the first place—proclamation, a message about God, but a way of living, a way of being in community, standing over against and existing alongside the normal ways of social life. The task of the Church, which basically is not to supply information, is "to perform those actions which generate christic expectation by way of experience as communal sharing. But this is frightening, because such experiences tend to become ecstatic."[24] Again, partly influenced by Turner, Driver underlines the importance of religious ritual as the mode effectively inducing such experience. Ritual provides the liminal experiences that give men and women a sense of freedom and of altered possibilities for life, of new ways of being and doing. In its repetition, occasion is provided for creativity with all it implies, for the dreaming of new dreams, the thinking of new thoughts and the moving into true community. So Driver argues that "Christ is Christ only within the *communitas* of worship," or again, "within the spaces of Christian ritual."[25] Here his thought reflects our earlier discussion of pilgrimage and processions with the

22 Ibid., p. 27.
23 Ibid., pp. 65-66.
24 Ibid., p. 148.
25 Ibid., pp. 165, 167.

difference between transnomic freedom (true liminality) and nomic reaffirmation (dramatic re-enactment of the past). In a fully liminal, ritual experience, Christ has an open character that is not restricted to functioning as centre or model. (When "Christ gravitates to the center-point of sacramental practice... even Spirit is routinized."[26]) But such a Christ stands in contrast to the Christ of status within a social structure. Moreover, Driver contends that in the real experience of Christian communitas, the focus is not upon Christ, God, or the Spirit. Nor is communitas primarily an experience of social, ecclesial, or religious hierarchy. Outside nomos may be anomy but there also lies the possibility of a highly sensitive communitas where ethical awareness is at its greatest.

Let me share some quotations from Driver where the language is expressive of the transnomic, speaking both of the nomic and of the need to move beyond it. He refers to "the memory of Christ past, while not rubbed out, being subordinate."[27] The transnomic, in my opinion, is aware of the need to recognize the necessary place of structure even while seeing the need to transcend it, to accept it as a launching pad or guidance but not as a resting place or limitation. Thus the transnomic both affirms and denies the nomos, a tension reflected in Driver. He speaks of the need of "not only the honoring but also the *betrayal* of the original."[28] He cites the challenge which comes from committed groups of Christians who "declare that they are going to *follow* him (like the disciples of old) *away* from present practice."[29] Even in the early Church itself, he finds this kind of allegiance, calling for transformation and rejection of elements of the tradition and its structures. Peter's breaking of the Jewish dietary laws and Paul's denial of the necessity of circumcision are cases in point. Seemingly, what Driver offers in *Christ in a Changing World* has the character of a transnomic Christology.

Let me now make some critical comments upon those trends within Driver's thought where I find roadblocks to a fully transnomic understanding. His Christology is, I believe, open to interpretation in ways which, if not anomic, are essentially only parabolic. Repudiating the imprisonment of Christian thought in the Christ past, he is in danger of devaluing the necessary role of the nomic.

Not unaware of the necessity for structure and order in human life, Driver knows the crucially important role of the past. While it

26 Ibid., p. 167.
27 Ibid., p. 134.
28 Ibid., p. 80 (his emphasis).
29 Ibid., p. 51 (his emphasis).

cannot provide an adequate framework for responding fully and creatively in the present-future, without some historical continuity, we would be in danger. So he refers to the scriptures as "our memory bank," commenting that "without them we would suffer institutional amnesia and go mad."[30] In fact, he writes of his own sense of anxiety in developing this Christology, lest he be lost in a wilderness of relativity and chaos. He is, therefore, at pains to stress that his adoption of relativity does not mean advocating moral relativism. One simply must condemn some things as wrong. The nomic has a valid place. Furthermore, he comments that "no one can live in a community of christic expectation all the time,"[31] that no one can live constantly in the anti-structural exuberance of communitas. Yet, significantly, he goes on to say that "the social world in which we are living is hostile to all authentic forms of community,"[32] as if structure, by its very nature, were hostile to nurturing anti-structure and freedom, to fostering communitas. Even if Driver is not claiming that all social worlds are antagonistic to true community, that it is merely a characteristic of our present situation, one may still ask whether this is not too simple. Are there no elements of the present social order relatively conducive to communitas? I suggest that he fails to give enough thought to the positive potential of the nomic in service of the transnomic.

Likewise, Driver criticizes a vast range of contemporary Christologies because of their self-binding to Christ past, without analyzing the extent to which some, in this binding, are nevertheless open to transcend that nomos even as they affirm it—to be transnomic Christologies, attuned to the valid role of the nomic. One must see in him an approach to the transnomic, articulated almost exclusively in the parabolic. With him we are apt to lose the necessary and creative role of the nomic, of being offered the anomic in place of the transnomic. He claims Tillich's Protestant principle, the dynamism in Luther and others, which rejects confinement by tradition. Unlike Tillich, however, Driver sees structure as essentially wrong, whereas Tillich stressed the necessity for a dynamic relationship between the Protestant principle and religious or Catholic substance, between anti-structure and structure. One finds a similar shift in Driver's reading of Turner. Correctly, he sees in Turner an understanding of society as processual, a rhythmic movement between structure and anti-structure, and of religious ritual as a dramatic means whereby society experi-

30 Ibid., p. 91.
31 Ibid., p. 148.
32 Ibid., p. 149.

ences the liminal, being lifted out of its nomic structures and enabled to envisage new possibilities. He stresses the dangers of religious ritual becoming domesticated, being forced into servitude of the nomos, either by letting off steam in ecstatic moments to reduce the pressure for change, or by powerfully reinforcing what is. Yet Turner did not see the nomic moment as simply negative, but as potentially creative in preserving the basic orders of society, thereby enhancing the possibility of the liminal moment and the experience of communitas. As he put it, mankind "*grows* through anti-structure and *conserves* through structure."[33] Consequently, it is contrary to Turner's understanding to say, as Driver implies, that social structures are inevitably counter to communitas. Structure *in se* is not communitas, but it need not be antithetical to communitas. For Turner, some structures obviously are more conducive to this experience than others and should be fostered by those who seek this experience.

One may approach this relation of the nomos to the liminal or transnomic not only in Turner's sociological categories but also in terms of the psychology of identity. Who is the Christ of whom Driver speaks? He can argue that the important question is who is Jesus today. What does it mean to call him Christ? What is our relationship to him, and what behaviour and expectations for the future does he evoke in us? What is the resurrected Christ doing in our modern world? Driver insists that we be concerned not with a Christ past but with a Christ future. He alludes to the ecstatic experience of communitas as an experience of the Christ, but who is this Christ? How would we recognize him unless it is by some reference to the Christ past? No matter how much we need transform, transcend, even partially repudiate, dimensions of the Christ past, nonetheless, the word "Christ" has no clear meaning without reference to the past, concretely to the Jesus of history. Driver says also that although we may have been granted some Christian revelation in the past, we cannot say God is bound by that revelation, that he cannot do something altogether new. But how would we know it was God unless it has some relationship to what we have already experienced as the Divine? What sense would it make to say that the God we have so experienced is the Christian God, for Christology has no content without the nomic? This merely substantiates Tillich's assertion that faith must have religious or Catholic substance, and this is true, even if our Christology would finally be transnomic.

33 Turner, *Dramas, Fields, and Metaphors*, p. 298 (his emphasis).

I find a kindred problem in Driver's discussion of personal identity. He tends to short-change the place of structure as part of the moral agent. His attack on the idolatry of the past leads him to formulate a different sense of time. Given his focus, he turns to the analysis of moral agency and sees the moral intention as the primary expression of humanness. This, in turn, draws attention to purposeful time, "present time oriented toward the future,"[34] or, as he prefers, human time is "present-future" time. How does one imagine the future? How does one envisage solutions to moral dilemmas? Driver suggests that inevitably we turn to memory, understanding the future by making proximate interpretations based upon the past, but that this memory of the past must remain in service to the present-future, rather than master it. True, except it creates the impression that the past only enters to serve the future in a moment of reflection when the moral agent has a problem. But how does the agent derive this intention in the first place? How does he/she acquire the initial orientation towards the present-future, if not in terms of an already appropriated past? Driver himself gives expression to this when he speaks of the "memoried context in which we live and act,"[35] agreeing with Berger and Luckmann who speak of the social construction of reality. Surely, if all knowing and perception is structured by the memoried past, then the crucial issue is whether the appropriated past, the socially constructed reality, in short, the nomos within, is supportive or destructive of our moral freedom and sensitivity. Driver inclines towards the same error as much situation ethics, placing great emphasis upon freedom and context but sounding, in the moment of decision, as if it were a naked ego entering the context to choose. This fails to take account of the identity of the moral agent, the law written upon the heart. While the nomos must not define the answer in advance, it is relevant in advance of a free answer. The nomos is not that simply from which we must break free; it also provides a structure to enhance or weaken moral agency. Driver's emphasis upon the parabolic—while perhaps a useful mechanism in shaking the easy rigidities of orthodoxy—is in danger of losing sight of this crucial factor.

Driver accentuates, in his Christology, our need to be sensitive to the idolatries of the past, of the rigid Christ who becomes a divisive, rather than a healing force, an instrument of christofascism. We must learn to be Christian without being *paternalistic*. I suggest, however,

34 Driver, *op. cit.*, p. 9.
35 Ibid., p. 29.

that in order to be *Christian* without being paternalistic, one must also struggle with the question of what it means to follow Christ, while leaving him free to be, free to transcend dramatically, at times even shockingly, our conceptualizations of him. How do we appropriate the Christian nomos in a manner supporting a transnomic experience and understanding?

Cobb's Renomic Theology

John B. Cobb, Jr., in *Christ in a Pluralistic Age*, offers another contemporary Christology which has a distinctly transnomic quality. Although his study is quite different from Driver's, Cobb, in many ways, is motivated by the same constellation of factors, namely, a deep concern that Christian theology must recognize the reality of pluralism and relativism in modern culture, an awareness of the dangers of Christian imperialism, and a conviction that we must consider the ethical consequences of our formulations.

"Two related factors of modern experience," Cobb writes, "the profane consciousness and pluralism, have played a dominant role in obscuring Christ."[36] The second of these, pluralism, is the more important for this work. In particular, Cobb desires Christian self-understanding in the presence of, and in relationship to, the other great world religions; of them, Buddhism attracts his primary attention. No longer can we simply assume that Christianity is the one and only true way. How then do we meaningfully proclaim loyalty to Christ, while recognizing the realities of pluralism and the relativity of all things?

Like Driver, Cobb is sensitive to the dangers of unqualified relativism. "The threat of relativism is the most critical issue the Christian pluralist has to face."[37] Nevertheless, he would side with H. Richard Niebuhr (in *The Meaning of Revelation*), declaring that this very relativism carries a positive potential for Christian understanding and the articulation of the faith. He actually argues that if we are properly to understand the meaning of Christ and that which Christ is about in our world, then "the Christian consciousness must be freed from its fear that to move forward in the acceptance of the secular and pluralistic world threatens its faithfulness to Christ."[38] He

36 John B. Cobb, Jr., *Christ in a Pluralistic Age* (Philadelphia: Westminster Press, 1975), p. 18.
37 Ibid., p. 59.
38 Ibid., p. 187.

maintains that it is equally necessary for secular consciousness to be freed from its fear that to acknowledge the spirit that is Christ as operative in itself is to betray its own critical and open spirit. (Clearly, the meaning of the Christ is raised in such assertions.) Cobb speaks of his work as entailing a "post-modern pluralistic method"[39] which calls for a pluralistic spirit relativizing many of the static options of past theology. While he does not submit the concept of relativity to the same detailed analysis as Driver, I suggest that he is equally sensitive and committed at this point.

Cobb is alert to the dangers of Christian theological imperialism. Speaking of attempts to reinterpret the Christ of the creeds, he comments:

> Unless great care is taken, Christians and others alike will hear the same imperialist claims in our assertions today. This can be checked only by a full recognition of the variety of structures of existence among which that of Jesus is one and that of Gautama, for example, is another. Only then can an account of Jesus as distinctively incarnating God leave open the question of the relative importance of that event in comparison with Gautama's enlightenment.[40]

In Cobb, unlike Driver, one does not sense the same burning passion and shared Christian guilt over the injustices of christofascism. Rather, there is a concern that this very exclusivist interpretation of Christ prevents the proper comprehension and appropriation of the Christian faith itself. The tendency to think of Jesus as the centre of meaning who, in some sense, therefore, stands in contrast to and against all other centres of meaning, simply does not meet the needs of today's Christian. We can no longer afford the purely negative views adopted in the past towards other world religions. Consequently, Cobb rejects Barth's interpretation of Christianity as the one, true, God-inspired faith—in contrast to the man-made religions of history. Cobb specifically seeks to enrich Christian understanding through an in-depth encounter with Buddhism. The Christian nomos can be enriched and fructified through the insights of the Buddhist. One might say that whereas Driver opposes Christian imperialism as a source of injustice to Jews, women, and others, Cobb rejects it in the form of Christian exclusivism, primarily because it distorts the self-understanding of Christians and limits their ability to appropriate the dynamic reality of the Christ.

39   Ibid., p. 15.
40   Ibid., p. 169.

> The thesis of this book is that faithfulness to Christ requires immersion in the secular and pluralistic consciousness and that it is precisely there that Christ now works, impeded by our failure to recognize him and by our continuing association of faith with past, particularized expressions of Christ.[41]

In the terms of this discussion, the issue of Christian imperialism becomes a matter of remaining faithful to the Christian nomos without dogmatically imposing this upon others.

Cobb's work reflects more of a desire to write a systematic, contemporary Christology than to agonize over ethical issues. Nevertheless, for him a powerful ethical imperative is operative, one pertaining to the very question of human survival on this endangered planet. Can Christians see their way beyond the exclusivism of traditional understandings, which so often have caused them to ride roughshod over others, and learn to work co-operatively with all people for the sake of the race? Thus in the latter portion of his book, Cobb seeks to articulate new images of Christian hope with which to guide the deliberations of mankind. Within the context of his systematic, theological work, he struggles to relate these images of hope to Christ as articulated in the earlier chapters. In all this we find sensitivity to the immediate realities of human need. Our visions of the future have often been ones which threaten the environment—if not life itself. We must recapture the biblical feeling for the whole of creation in God's plan. "Images of hope for human beings alone betray an exaggerated estimate of the separability of our species from the rest of creation and of God's exclusive preoccupation with us."[42] They also betray an unchristian indifference to other forms of life, all too characteristic of our history.

Cobb and Driver have similar concerns. Yet with Cobb, they find their place in the theologian's systematic understanding of the Christ. Hence his movement towards the transnomic will have less of the tone of a prophetic attack on the inadequacies of present theologies, Driver's parabolic emphasis, and more of an attempt to rethink the Christ image, to renomize the faith. In so doing, however, it too manifests a transnomic flavour.

Of course, Cobb's writings still reflect at various points the parabolic, the pure critique of the mythic, nomic, or structural dimensions of Christian understanding. Reminiscent of the writings of John Crossan, he refers to the parabolic character of Christ's teachings, to

41 Ibid., p. 187.
42 Ibid., p. 255.

"the unsettling encounter with the words of Jesus." He cites, for example, the parable of the Pharisee and the publican. "To hear this story is to see values reversed. If one's sense of values is not turned upside down, he has not heard the message."[43] However, given the different emphasis in Cobb's discussion, one finds less of the strongly parabolic than occurs in Driver. In fact, he goes on quickly to offer a mythoparabolic image of the parables. "Jesus' words not only reverse or tear down the hearer's world; they can also build up a world and give the hearer a place to stand."[44] Like Driver, nonetheless, Cobb clearly recognizes the dangers of idolatry of the past, of nomic bondage. He refers to the tendency of so many Christians to believe "that their faith requires the absolutization of the particular in their history rather than its confession as particular."[45] They seek absolute assurance, some sort of proof, rather than admit the historical and particular anchorage of a faith which can only be confessed. Barth, in Cobb's opinion, is a powerful exponent of this tendency. He led theology to a reaffirmation and study of its own tradition which ignored the emerging claims of other traditions. Once more we find the attempt to establish nomic security, a security purchased at the price of nomic bondage. Emphasis was on the past, away from the future or present-future where ethical decisions must be made: "the focus of Christian attention was redirected from the future to the past. The supernatural fact of Jesus as God was located at a particular point in the past."[46] But surely the Christian must look, not backward to Driver's "dead" Christ, but to Christ as the new, the yet-to-be, the coming, divine reality. We must be free from bondage to tradition, thereby relativizing all that is past and accomplished. For Cobb, all human understanding rests upon a nomic foundation, upon an interpretation of reality, and thus it is unrealistic, indeed impossible, to think of shedding the past. The issue is that of ending our bondage to the past, ceasing to absolutize it, for such bondage limits our capacity to respond fully to the call of God in the present.

Cobb develops his discussion of nomic bondage by drawing a distinction between faith and the sacred. Faith, when true and alive, is transnomic. When it is sacralized, it loses its freedom of expression, its vitality, and becomes rigidly fixed by its traditional forms of conceptualization; it is in bondage to its own past form. When the creeds were translated into dogma, Christ was transformed into a stultified, sacred object in reference to which the ordinary, critical and scholarly

43   Ibid., pp. 115, 108.
44   Ibid., p. 110.
45   Ibid., p. 49.
46   Ibid., p. 164.

question was out of place. "He was to be worshipped rather than studied or even encountered."[47] As Christ and Christian faith developed into absolutes, simultaneously other religions were held to be in error. Using Driver's terms, Christ became solely Christ past while Christ of the present-future, open and dynamic, was lost. Theology's task, in consequence, is to break this correlation of faith and the sacred.

This conviction is reflected at two significant points in Cobb's discussion: his treatment of theology's development, especially in modern times, and his analysis of the relationship between faith and reason. In the history of theology he finds the long, Christian tradition which associated faith with the sacred. The vehicles or foci of faith, be they tradition, the Jesus of history or holy writ, became unquestioned, sacred objects, the religious world-taken-for-granted. A study of world religions, however, which came to prominence in the nineteenth century through increased contact with other cultures, broke this automatic and immediate "twinning" of faith with the Christian sacred. Christianity began to be seen as one religion among others, and religion as a part of culture, which inevitably led to a recognition of the historical and cultural relativity of all religious understanding. The correlation between the theologian's faith and his sacred objects was thus superseded by the relativizing of all sacred forms. The rupture of this relationship made possible, for the first time, an appreciation by Christian thinkers of the value of other religious traditions. Christ, as the divine, could no longer be identified exclusively with any form determined by past doctrines. For Cobb, this meant a new imaging of Christ and a creative transformation of theology itself. But theology can only fulfill this mandate when it breaks the absolute correlation between the theologian's faith and its past expressions, when it refuses to sacralize its own nomos.

In his brief discussion of faith and reason, Cobb states that all too often faith has been seen as unverifiable assumptions about reality with the associated commitments. Reason, by contrast, has been assumed to be the clearly objective, neutral, detached reflection upon life, free from any commitments. Our modern awareness, however, makes it clear that this distinction is indefensible. No interpretation of reality, no so-called rational conception, is free from the necessarily unverifiable starting points of thought. All reason rests upon faith. Furthermore, all true faith must allow itself to remain open to the inquiring, reforming, purging impact of criticial reflection. Faith

47 Ibid.

and reason, rather than vying with each other, are actually united in the struggle against idolatry. "The reason which is faith is disciplined imagination."[48] When faith is opposed to reason, when faith is identified as the sacred nomos beyond criticism, then we discover ourselves in bondage, with these two factors in conflict. "Faith as vision of reality is the indispensible context for reason, but if any one vision of reality is absolutized or sacralized, it inhibits the fullest development and use of reason."[49] Every interpretation of reality, Cobb stresses, including that which his is developing, must be open to critical examination and reformation: "the faith that supports the pluralistic consciousness must oppose its own sacralization."[50] All nomoi must be recognized as transcendable. Faith must not be identified with a sacred truth. For Cobb, as for Driver, theology must never operate on the basis of a sacred and unassailable structure or mythos. For the Christian, the question is how to conceive of faith against a backdrop of desacralization. Are there only two alternatives—either a return to the rigidly nomized faith of a Karl Barth or an uncommitted relativism? For Cobb the answer is no. Christian faith can only live again as faith, when it breaks its correlation with the sacred.

One senses a major difference in emphasis and approach between Cobb and Driver. Obviously Cobb recognizes the existence, the inevitability, and even the creative potential of structure in human existence. At no time are we free from the formative influence of our internalized understandings, our visions of reality. In much contemporary rethinking of the Christian faith, he finds a new normative structure, taken from other than Christian understanding and experience. Richard Rubenstein's *My Brother Paul* offers what he regards as an interesting new perspective upon Paul's experience, which raises useful insights and asks valuable questions. Nevertheless, what one discovers is that the normative perspective in the work is Freudian theory. Freud has become the sacred, the absolutized and unchallenged norm for interpreting the Apostle. Rubenstein no more escapes the influence of his presuppositions than did Christian interpreters in the past. Unlike Cobb and Driver, however, he seems less critically aware of his presuppositions, the nomos within which he is operating, and hence, he is less free, perhaps from the effects of bondage. His analysis fails to be adequately self-critical. Against this Cobb asserts:

48 Ibid., p. 93.
49 Ibid., p. 91.
50 Ibid.

a theological treatment based on a truly contemporary, and therefore broken or desacralized, relation to Paul can be at least as objective as a Freudian one. The distinction is that the theological approach locates itself in a history that continues to be normatively affected by the liberating effects of Paul's teaching instead of a history that is normatively determined by Freud.[51]

Although, for Cobb, the call remains to find a transnomic stance in faith, some freedom over against tradition, it yet remains critical to consider what is the sacred past from which we are emerging, what vision of reality is operative in our reflections. Assuredly, this is not a problem that theologians find only in Rubenstein's analysis of Paul. Contemporary Christian eschatology, attempting to develop images of hope with which to guide faith's journey into the future, is often trapped too in allegiance to "the dominant but dying modern consciousness,"[52] to secular visions which rule out, *a priori*, many dimensions of the Christian hope.

While recognizing that Christ can be understood in a repressive manner, the opposite danger of anomy, the abandonment of all norms and the acceptance of unqualified pluralism, cannot be accepted by the Christian. No one lives without norms. Christians must continue, if their identity is to remain Christian, to find that which is supremely important, bound up in some significant way, with Jesus of Nazareth: "no other image is identical with Christ, and theology itself cannot abandon its concern for just that image."[53] To be Christian and transnomic is to be sure that it is the *Christian* nomos one is transcending, that it is *Christian* structure from which one is emerging. As we shall see, in his Christology, Cobb develops an important distinction between Christ and Jesus, but clearly it is the Jesus of history and his story which most powerfully shape our image of the Christ and, in turn, the language and vision of the Church. To be Christian is to stand in a vital relationship with Driver's Christ past.

A perennial tension in the history of Christian thought is that between loyalty to the Christian experience of Jesus and to understandings of God and human nature derived from other sources. Witness, for example, the powerful role played by Greek philosophy in shaping the early evolution of Christian doctrine. In Cobb's opinion, we must be certain that the structure to which we adhere—without being enslaved—is found in Jesus. "If it is in Jesus that we

51 Ibid., p. 53.
52 Ibid., p. 182.
53 Ibid., p. 20.

perceive what God's immanence is and does, then it is from Jesus that we should learn what God is like. We can and must reverse the long history of retaining ideas of God uncongenial to what is apparent in Jesus."[54] Cobb feels that nowadays we have less assurance in our faith, owing, in part, to the fact that the Christ reality has broken free from Christian history and has become powerfully diffused throughout the whole human experience. Precisely in such a time as this, Christians need study the historical Jesus. We must recognize the importance of our determining vision, a vision found in Jesus of Nazareth as the Christ. The latter is crucial not only in providing the perspective from which we interpret life, but also in directing us towards those moments that were formative for the first Christians. Moreover, Cobb argues that by acknowledging Jesus as normative, the way is prepared, from bondage to the past, to true fulfillment. The Christian nomos is a preparation for the transnomic. To heed the words of Jesus increases their power to lead us into the truth. Longing to be in Christ helps actualize its consummation. The vision of hope, bound up with the Lord, opens us to creative appropriation of the future. Yet, law, as nomos, is a foundation for the gospel, as transnomic.

Cobb deals with this dynamic at some length in relation to conscience, insisting that it is important to understand it from a Christian perspective where it is seen as an encounter with the Christ. Such an image encourages us not to think of conscience as a personal possession or attribute. Far from being a rigid following of some formal moral principle, it is a sensitive openness to the Christ, not only to the demand for transformation, which can be threatening, but also to an accepting and creative love.[55] To think of conscience in this way is "to express and to elicit trust. . . . In short, it is to call for and make possible radical conversion from bondage to the past to openness to the future."[56]

Thus, in contrast to Driver, Cobb stresses the importance of the nomic. No one can live without some sort of structuring, ordering reality. The issue is whether or not we are oriented by a structure that is healing and creative, one that opens the way to move beyond itself to the freedom of the children of God.

Schematically, Driver offers a Christology with a transnomic character, approached through a basic emphasis upon the parabolic

54 Ibid., p. 168.
55 Cf. the discussion of the transmoral conscience in the previous chapter.
56 Cobb, *Christ in a Pluralistic Age*, p. 85.

or anti-structural; Cobb, on the other hand, offers a transnomic Christology through an emphasis upon the rearticulation of the nomos, what one might call the *renomic* rather than the parabolic. The meaning and reality of Christ is not finally settled by the past, by the decrees of bishops, councils, or theologians. Rather, it evolves with the articulation of images that clarify and deepen the present experience of the resurrected Lord. Christ does not mean for us today precisely what Christ meant for the first-century Christians. Ours is a different world. Thus, in a sense, Christology has a history of change and development—a thought immediately compatible with Cobb's process philosophy. Yet he would argue that this claims nothing unusual, for throughout Christian history, the Christ image has continually been renomized. The christological debates of the first centuries were an attempt to rethink and re-express the understanding of the faith. Bonhoeffer's description of Jesus as "the man for others," liberation theologians who see him identifying with the oppressed, black theologians, feminist theologians, all proffer counter-mythic Christologies. The crucial point, according to Cobb, is that, as we encounter and reflect upon the Incarnate One, we come to understand that our Christology must constantly be renomized. "Precisely through deepening its central conviction of incarnation, Christian faith moves toward its own transformation through openness to all faiths."[57] Who, then, is this renomized Christ? What is the new image of the Nazarene which impels us towards a transnomic understanding?

We here cannot submit Cobb's renomized Christology to a full critical analysis, but let us clarify the understanding of theology and the theological task implicit in this work, defending the claim that it entails a transnomic conception. (I shall only sketch his thesis, pointing out its implications.)

Cobb argues that the word "Christ" has a wide context of meaning, defined with reference to other terms with broad connotations. It is not, therefore, properly susceptible to a narrow, highly specific, and limited definition. Such is characteristic of the great words from all religious traditions. These images "have as their referents vast and changing clusters of meanings."[58] The theological task is to guide the responsible development of images, to prevent their wandering into perversion and error. Specifically, the concept of the Christ has a dual reference, to God and to Jesus, each of which

57 Ibid., p. 24.
58 Ibid., p. 65.

has a complex significance. "'Christ' does not designate Jesus as such but refers to Jesus in a particular way, namely, as the incarnation of the divine. It does not designate deity as such but refers to deity experienced as graciously incarnate in the world."[59] In the development of his Christology, Cobb begins by articulating an understanding of the Christ as the Logos, re-imaging this as "creative transformation." He then proceeds, in the second section of the work, to maintain that such a Christ-logos is validly and meaningfully related to the Jesus of history. The first portion, discussing Christ as creative transformation, focuses upon Christ in our present experience, so he suggests, while reflection upon Christ and the historical Jesus directs to the past. In the third part, he turns to Christ and the future, seeking to re-image the Christian understanding of the future in terms of Christ as creative transformation.

How do we understand the Christ to be present and active in our world? More especially, how do we understand God to be there, given our contemporary experience of a profane, secular, and pluralistic consciousness? Cobb directs us to "the image of [Christ as] creative transformation."[60]

The study begins with an account of "Christ as Creative Transformation in Art," drawing upon the work of André Malraux. Malraux contends that Christ has disappeared from the content of art. Modern artists increasingly give their allegiance to an inner sense of power to interpret and transform reality. In brief, Malraux's thesis is that Western art began with Christ represented in essential divinity, with Jesus as God, but gradually the image became humanized and incarnate. Thereafter, art became progressively more interested in individual men and women, an interest that Cobb maintains is in keeping with the christified understanding of human nature in Christian faith. Finally, artists developed a heightened and personalized sense of their own unique selfhood. Cobb accepts this basic historical data, proposing, however, that "as Christ disappeared from the content of Western art he became, under other names, its acknowledged inner principle."[61] While no longer its subject, Christ remains its inner dynamic and meaning. Cobb refers to Malraux's own assertion that modern art must finally progress to the point where it relativizes art itself. Cobb sees this trend in art as identical with the creative transformation that is life. No form, only creative transformation, is abso-

59 Ibid., p. 66.
60 Ibid., p. 21.
61 Ibid., p. 31.

lute. Malraux, in effect, recognizes as the inner dynamic of art the expression of a broader reality, and this reality Cobb would name as the Christ, the Logos.

> The recognition that this power is not the power of art alone but of all life leads the artist to demystify art and destroy the boundaries between it and creative activity in general. It is now time for the Christian boldly to name as Christ what has for so long been separated from that name.[62]

Similarly, Cobb traces a process of creative transformation in the history of modern Christian theology, the process being initiated through its encounter with world religions. The latter revealed Christianity as a relative phenomenon, relative to its own time and cultural setting. Under the impact of objective study, a creative transformation of theology has shattered the correlation of faith and the sacred, opening Christian thought to the dynamic reality of pluralism and moving it into a transnomic space. "Christ is not to be identified with any given form established by past doctrine but instead with the creative transformation of theology that has broken our relationship to every established form."[63]

To this point, Cobb has simply sketched what he views as an inner dynamic, producing a radical change in both art and theology. He acknowledges, however, that one can hardly be content to call this the Logos, unless it corresponds to an ontological reality, and one not simply operative in art and theology. "If creative transformation is Christ, it must be discernible in all life."[64] To establish the ontological and universal status of Logos as creative transformation, to justify the assertion that this reality is divine, Cobb draws upon Whitehead's process metaphysics. He speaks of the interaction or tension at every moment between efficient and final causation, "between the influence of the past and the lure of the future."[65] In Whiteheadian terms, this is a constant element of every actual occasion. This lure of the future is the initial aim of the occasion, a call into fuller, redemptive, whole being. This is the inner dynamic of reality *in se*. So Cobb can describe the Logos as "the order of unrealized potentiality making possible by its immanence the realization of novel order."[66] The name "Christ," in this context, refers to the immanence or incarnation of this principle in the world of living things and particularly of human beings. (To be sure, Cobb suggests that ultimately we must

62 Ibid., p. 43.
63 Ibid., p. 61.
64 Ibid., p. 63.
65 Ibid., p. 67.
66 Ibid., p. 75.

recognize the Logos as operative in the inanimate as well, otherwise life itself could not be said to have emerged under the call of God.) The word "Christ" connotes this power of creative transformation in the world and claims for it a divine status. Thus his fundamental re-imaging of the Christ portrays him as the divine, present in a creative transformation operative throughout the whole of reality, but particularly recognized by Christians in a human life.

In what sense can we say that this power was incarnate in Jesus of Nazareth? Is it defensible to claim that he was the power of creative transformation personified? Or have we proclaimed another god? Only if we can say that the Logos as creative transformation is discernibly incarnate in the Galilean, do we have a renomizing of Christology, for as Cobb admits, in a formal sense, Christ denotes that which Christians recognize as supremely important in the Jesus of history. Assuredly, he is not trying to prove that the Logos was incarnate in this man. Such would be an attempt to sacralize and move out of the categories of true faith. Cobb feels, though, that it is not inconsistent to think of him in terms of creative transformation.

To vindicate this, he draws upon four contemporary studies of Jesus' life (another return to the historical figure at this uncertain time), including one by a Marxist atheist, Milan Machovec. Each sees Jesus as producing a creative transformation in the Judaism of his own day. Moreover, his teachings still have this creative and transforming impact upon us, one which could be described as parabolic. This Cobb understands as being central: "The conclusion is that the encounter with Jesus' words even today is an experience of creative transformation, or, otherwise stated, that Jesus' words can be the occasion for the deepening of the incarnation or the fuller realization of Christ."[67] Consequently, it does no violence to the image of Jesus in the New Testament to find in him an expression of creative transformation which continues to influence those who encounter him, both in his words and through the community of faith. But, of course, Cobb admits, his own Whiteheadian understanding of the Logos as the initial aim means that this reality is, in fact, in all persons. In what sense can we say that it was peculiarly present in Jesus, making meaningful the claim that he was the incarnate Christ? Again it is not a matter of proof but is it rationally meaningful? Once more, the answer is in process terms, particularly in its understanding of the self, not in substantial but relational categories. The self is the focusing and ordering centre which receives the experiences of the past and

67 Ibid., p. 99.

reaches out towards the possibilities of the future. In these terms, it is meaningful to say that the self of Jesus could be constituted by the Logos. In such a structure of existence:

> the presence of the Logos would share in constituting selfhood; that is, it would be identical with the center or principle in terms of which other elements in experience are ordered. In that structure the appropriation of one's personal past would be just that ideal appropriation made possible by the lure of creative novelty that is the immanent Logos.[68]

Cobb suggests that this possibility was a reality in Jesus of Nazareth, so that when he spoke it was God speaking also. Nevertheless, he remained a fully human person with all the particularities of his unique, human past, being drawn into the reality of that self at any moment. My purpose, let me stress, is not to enter into any detailed critique of Cobb's position but merely to outline his argument that the Christ conceived as creative transformation can be seen as a continuation or expression of that reality which has been the focus of Christian understanding, namely, the incarnate Christ, the event of Jesus of Nazareth.

Cobb ends his study by discussing the implications of his thesis for our conceptualization of the future. In keeping with his emphasis upon the importance of the nomic, he feels it is crucially important that we create images of the future which are open or, in our terms, transnomic, and which invoke in us an expectation of the power of creative transformation. Only with these can we live hopefully and creatively. With the Christian understanding of the Christ as creative transformation, we dare to live confidently in the face of the undetermined future, "for we know that the principle of this indeterminacy is the creative transformation we trust as Christ"[69] and we also recognize that Christ as love. So Cobb concludes his work with a series of images of the future—with a model of the new city drawn from the work of Paolo Soleri, for example. He offers these as proximate visions to which we may dedicate ourselves, aware that that dedication must include the freedom to transcend them.

Can we call this a transnomic theology? I would answer clearly in the affirmative. Cobb concedes, much more than Driver, the important, creative place of structure and the resultant necessity to delineate the Christian nomos. The image he offers, however, is one which repeatedly invokes the necessity to transcend it. The Logos, in

68 Ibid., p. 139.
69 Ibid., p. 183.

much Christian thought, tends to be associated with order, structure, and rational cohesion, whereas in Cobb it is seen as continuous rethinking, as creative transformation, breaking our relationship to all established forms, in short, transnomic. His repeated call to sever the connection between faith and the sacred, his assertion that our very allegiance to the true nomos prepares the way for that experience which transcends it, marks his thought as *trans*nomic rather than anomic. The Christ is creative transformation, yet also incarnate in Jesus of Nazareth. More than Christology, this is an understanding that changes the conception of all theology. "He [Christ] . . . breaks the relation to himself as objectified figure and becomes the principle of liberation at work in theology itself."[70]

Having said that, let us recognize in Cobb's approach a danger to which we should be alerted. Whereas Driver's emphasis upon the parabolic left him susceptible to the charge of being anomic, of devaluing structure, Cobb's attempt to renomize Christology could have us end in bondage to our new imaging. (He himself is sensitive to this possibility.) Moreover, those who do not find Whitehead and process thought convincing may question whether Cobb has bound Christian faith too closely to this philosophical nomos. Is his image of the Christ as creative transformation more crucially informed by Whitehead than the New Testament? Has his emphasis upon creative transformation lost sight of the power of Christ as creative preservation? Whatever our response, we cannot but see that in seeking a transnomic theology by renomizing, we may achieve merely the nomic in a new guise.

Story and Transnomic Theology

The Christologies developed by Driver and Cobb represent a move towards the transnomic. Each directly confronts the issue of nomic bondage at the point of highest significance, the Christian understanding of Jesus of Nazareth. While Driver's emphasis is upon the parabolic and Cobb's upon the counter-mythic, each writes with a lively sense of the transnomic as critical reflection in service of the nomic. One could argue that for Driver the criticism tends to outweigh the service, but this was the point he felt compelled to stress. Neither writer, however, fully succeeds in producing a transnomic theology. Such would constantly remind readers to criticize what they are reading. (Undoubtedly, both authors would

---

70 Ibid., p. 58.

covet this.) Moreover, it would invoke the experience and awareness that transcend all structures, including those of theology itself. The point, I believe, is less a matter of error in content than a matter of inadequacy of style; it is not so much what they say as how they say it. Our quest, then, is for a theology transnomic in style as well as substance.

If theology is to be fully transnomic, it is not sufficient for it to be self-critical, continually re-evaluating and restating its nomos. It is not enough to be sensitive to the dangers of unintentional errors in content. Driver reminds us, for example, that to speak of God as *Father* and redemption through *his son* can lead to a devaluation of women, and of the feminine in men. I suggest that our theology has failed if it does not also evoke a sense of mystery and a call to a spiritual adventure which lies beyond the security of doctrinal formulation. The test of an appropriate statement of faith cannot be simply that it proclaims the truth (develops a nomos) in a way which does not lead into nomic error. Theology must seek to lead men and women into mature and dynamic living, into a sense of the transnomic. We fail, in our endeavour to clarify and specify the structures of faith, if we only protect ourselves against a theology with a wrong effect, and do not strive for the full effect of a theology leading beyond itself. Theologies must define the nomos but they must also beckon to the transnomic.

Aarne Siirala claims that theology must become a participant in articulating the language of healing and transformation.

> Most endeavours of the various disciplines—theology included—to articulate a language of transformation end up being long on diagnosis, on the articulation of the disorganization of life, and short on prognosis, on the articulation of the dynamics of healing and transformation.[71]

Part of the problem of prognosis is that it requires more than articulating visions of health and ideal goals, such as Cobb suggests for society. It also depends upon the awakening of a transnomic attitude towards that very theology. Traditional theology has been long on clarifying the nomos, but short on evoking the transnomic. Where then do we look? Let me propose a narrative form of theologizing.

We have already noted the fact that storytelling has a long and significant place in religion, and have cited its potential as a means of individual and group transformation in psychotherapy and social process. While the social sciences cannot determine the content of

---

71 Siirala, "Theology and the unconscious," p. 622.

faith, they may throw light upon effective forms of our confession and cause us to give serious consideration to religion's storied past. Let me, therefore, simply recall and underline some of the characteristics of storytelling that are suggestive of the place of narrative form in developing a transnomic theology. (Thereafter, I will briefly review the work of Sallie McFague who, from a literary and biblical perspective, also points to transnomic theology as being less systematic and conceptual, more symbolic and narrative.)

Story, with its power to transform, has probably remained a vital element in religion for many reasons. Its usefulness, as a memory aid in preliterate cultures and as an enchanting diversion, has undoubtedly contributed to its vitality. Men and women live in their stories; they are wounded or healed by them. If religion seeks not just to inform but to heal, if its goal is not merely to impart holy facts about God but to engender free and vibrant living before him, if religion is truly a means of ultimate transformation, then narrative will continue to have a powerful place as an instrumentality of faith. Storytelling is not only for the immature, for our children. It remains vital for everyone, for the oft neglected Child within. It could be that the healing of our Child by story is always a necessary part in the rebirth of the total person. Even here, "a little child shall lead them." Theology must examine its relationship to experiencing and fostering transforming narrative. Gerhard von Rad remarks, "Perhaps our understanding of the Old Testament would be better if we were accustomed more often to theologize the art of simple telling and listening to stories."[72]

An examination of storytelling in counseling and social process provides a number of insights with implications for the development of a fully transnomic theology. Some aspects of storytelling support the work of the transnomic in service of the nomic, while others call to the experience of the transnomic itself. I shall cite four.

It is theology's task to articulate, as far as language will allow, the truths of revelation. Religion must speak; the faithful must bear witness, even if it is only the private witness of their inner thoughts concerning God. We are challenged to do this in a way that avoids the dangers of dogmatism, of nomic bondage, without falling into an empty relativism, the chaos of anomy. We are called to give guidance for Christian living while avoiding the perils of doctrinal arrogance. We must cultivate "open systems,"[73] as Wainwright terms them. This

72 Gerhard von Rad, *God at Work in Israel* (Nashville: Abingdon, 1980), p. 59.
73 Geoffrey Wainwright, *Doxology, The Praise of God in Worship, Doctrine and Life* (New York: Oxford University Press, 1980), pp. 435-38.

we have identified as a need for the transnomic in service of the nomic, for the continual criticism of our theology by standing apart from our doctrines, for Tillich's Protestant principle in service of Catholic substance. We seek forms for the expression of faith that can carry a rich content, yet in their style remind us that God transcends that content. Narrative told and enacted is such a literary genre.

We have seen that narrative in therapy can convey complex and even patient-specific meanings (the word of God spoken to the individual). Yet most therapists resist the temptation to interpret the story, to draw out its moral, as if there were but one correct meaning. Its very power to convey many layers of meaning turns story into a self-transcending message. The invitation to play and fantasize within a story world invites us to accept it not with a fixity which turns saga into servitude, ballad into bondage. This is the enriching experience of many forms of contemporary therapy, especially those which have developed the art of fantasizing. Turner, too, has shown us that the enacted stories found in rituals and ceremonies are able to convey both structure and anti-structure in the same drama, the definitions of a society concomitant with an invitation to transcend them: "metaphors of iconoclasm exist *within* the texture of ceremonies heavily endowed with icons."[74] Story can be didactic and disruptive simultaneously, bearing witness to some ways of seeing reality, while inviting the listener to experiment with its substance to find fuller, perhaps even different, meanings. To use Crossan's terminology, story is at once mythic and parabolic. This dual quality is more immediate and natural in narrative than in abstract, conceptual forms of expression and, in this sense, it is a fuller witness to divine mystery than are doctrinal statements. To be sure, one may suffocate this freedom by a confining literalism that turns poetry into science and drama into dogmatism. Allowed to be, however, story is mythoparabolic, structure and anti-structure, predetermined message and free fantasy in one event.

Story also is particularly effective at formulating the beginnings of order, a partial nomos, in periods of uncertainty when individual and societal identities are confused. Turner speaks of "liminal periods" in human history, claiming that ours may well be such a time. Sallie McFague makes a similar suggestion: "The Christian symbolic universe does not hold together for most of us."[75] In our

---

74 Turner, *Dramas, Fields, and Metaphors*, p. 295 (his emphasis).
75 Sallie McFague, *Speaking in Parables* (Philadelphia: Fortress Press, 1975), p. 106.

Towards a Transnomic Theology / 155

day, theology must seek to articulate the faith in a social setting where many cannot as yet appropriate much of the traditional Christian imagery, where many of the symbols ring no bells. A narrative form of theology, as McFague asserts, can offer mini-nomoi, so to speak, partial structures, short stories within which one can find a foothold whence to begin the adventure of faith. "It may be that parable [here defined as short, revelatory stories, set in ordinary life], while itself a story of a certain kind, is a more appropriate genre for our time, for unlike more developed narratives it does not call for the same degree of faith in cosmic or even societal ordering."[76] Patients in counseling do not put the whole of life together in one moment but, in a particular therapeutic interaction (a mini-drama) or in the recounting of some past moment (a personal vignette), they may discover a narrative framework that begins to bring meaning and order to some one portion of life. A society, in its rituals and ceremonies, may reinforce some important strand in the group's identity and sense of worth, proving to be an anchor in times of social uncertainty. Possibly a capacity to create mini-theologies, religious short stories, may be the challenge for theology at this time. If we would take seriously our need to evoke the experience of the transnomic, then, where necessary, we must perform the prior task of assisting in the birth of nomic order. Just as therapy gives a secure base of identity before the patient and counselor can play together, so, in liminal periods, we must create a nomic launching pad for the flight of faith into the transnomic.

Let me now suggest a third dimension of story which relates, in one sense, like the other two, to the service of nomic development, but, in another, to the creation of transnomic experience. In a way not open to the traditional articulation of theology, storytelling and fantasy speak to our psychic depths. In psychoanalytic terminology, they understand and communicate with both the conscious and the unconscious. Alternatively, the concept of a bicameral mind suggests that we should think of two modes of consciousness, one rational, verbal, and linear, the other holistic and symbolic, but again it is fantasy and story which each can hear. Both psychological perspectives are reflected in Turner's discussion of the transforming power of ritual liminality. Much that depth psychology sees as repressed into the unconscious emerges, so he believes, in liminal rituals and their associated myths.[77] Moreover, he feels that liminality can release

76 Ibid., p. 141.
77 Turner, *Dramas, Fields, and Metaphors*, p. 257.

symbols which "perpetually outstrip the possibilities of linguistic (and other cultural) expressions," a new logic behind which may lie "a fundamental structure of human mentality or even of the human brain itself."[78] Our lives are governed, our responses and attitudes shaped, our hopes and fears captured in the two "languages." The healing of the mind requires that each be addressed; likewise, the healing and transformation of the spirit which is salvation. If theology seeks to enunciate the Word of God, it cannot be content to declare that Word in a manner that addresses only half the person. The language of ultimate transformation must speak to all dimensions of the psyche. Through the hearing and telling of stories, we can experience such reality as may be said to cut "more keenly than any two-edged sword, piercing as far as the place where life and spirit, joints and marrow, divide" (Heb. 4:12). Storytelling challenges the tendency in theology to become overly abstract and rationalistic, to speak only to the intellect and forget the heart. Again, one may conceive of this as serving nomic formulation, in this instance the development of a richer nomic structure which includes symbolic and poetic, as well as rational and discursive, modes of understanding. Or, indeed, it may be that here we are brought into contact with the dimension of mind that lives in a more childlike, playful manner, resisting the temptation to mastery and entering joyfully into the transnomic.

Let me turn to one further narrative element which seems so clearly to express the transnomic *in se*. Both psychotherapy and social process reveal the priority of experience over interpretation; the experience itself is, finally, the more informative and transformative. The interpretation of that experience, while useful as guidance, is secondary to the experience itself. Despite his bias towards the rational and conceptual, Freud came to accept the crucial fact that it was not intellectual insight but working through an experience, in a process of re-experiencing, that healed. Progoff and others have noted that when patients begin to interpret their fantasies, the story is interrupted (a shift in cerebral hemispheres?) and the healing stops. Thus he calls for psyche-evoking rather than psychoanalysis. When one turns to the work of Grimes and Turner, the force of experience over interpretation is obvious. In the life of a people, social structures are reinforced or disrupted not through the study of ceremonials but through participation in them. It is following in the processions of La Conquistadora or actively joining in the re-enactment of the Entrada

---

78 Ibid., pp. 240-41.

that strengthens the religious and civic identity of Santa Fe. It was the experience of a pilgrimage that became a disruptive and potentially threatening force in medieval society. In short, experience, not detached observation and interpretation, is the primary sustaining and transforming power in human life. Participation, rather than mastery, is the secret of truth, healing, and growth. In theological context, we are saved by being caught up in the gracious movement of God, not by writing systematic theologies. Aarne Siirala warns of the distortion of human life and of theology that results from our Faustian consciousness. Too often we assume that we are given "a mandate from God to gain control of this world."[79] Theology then becomes an expression of man, the detached observer, who gains dominion through his unbiased, objective knowledge of reality. (I expect that many feminists would agree that "man" is the correct word in that sentence.) Such theology cannot heal because it offers a false understanding of our healing. By contrast, a theology of story or a narrative form of theologizing would invite us to play, fantasize, and participate rather than to work, control, and remain detached. Dennis Jaffe, in his writings, stresses our need to follow the law of "passive volition." "Don't try, just let it happen."[80] Winnicott talks of the importance of experiencing "a non-purposive state."[81] Story, I maintain, is a medium more attuned to grace than to mastery. The call for participation beckons to a transnomic appropriation of the faith, not nomic mastery, to adventurous involvement rather than the security of certain dogmas.

What would be the shape of a theology alive to narrative, to the transnomic, to psyche-(spirit) evoking? In her book, *Speaking in Parables*, Sallie McFague proposes some of its attributes, some of the directions which must infuse the work of narrative theologians. One might say that she offers some nomic beacons to guide us in our efforts. She calls for an "intermediary or parabolic theology—a theology that is, on the one hand, not itself parable and, on the other hand, not systematic theology, but a kind of theology which attempts to stay close to the parables."[82]

McFague does not employ the term "parable" with the same connotation given it by Crossan. In fact, she regards the Good Samaritan, Crossan's parable par excellence, not as a parable at all

---

79 Siirala, "Theology and the unconscious," p. 610.
80 Jaffe, *Healing From Within*, p. 197.
81 Winnicott, *Playing and Reality*, p. 55.
82 McFague, *Speaking in Parables*, p. 3.

but simply as an example story where the full meaning is found within the tale itself. She defines parable as revelatory narrative that conveys a meaning transcending the actual story itself, although one which can only be discovered through the medium of the story. Moreover, in the moment of its reception, the meaning is to some degree disruptive. To use the Crossan connotations, parables for McFague are mythic narratives which, because of the dramatic nature of their message, have as well the parabolic impact of a startling counter-myth. To her, parables speak lightly or indirectly about God by speaking directly of this world. They are, at one and the same time, religious and secular. In this dual reference they become extended metaphors, linking two worlds, which is the basis of their revelatory power for, as she asserts, "new meaning is always metaphorical . . . *there is no way now or ever to have strange truth directly.*"[83] Yet in the very power of revelation, they become shocking, disruptive, "parabolic." "If the listener or reader 'learns' what the parable has to 'teach' him or her, it is more like a shock to the nervous system than it is like a piece of information to be stored in the head."[84] Parables, then, are a means of revelation and transformation. We have in them "a form that insists on uniting language, belief, and life—the words in which we confess our faith, the process of coming to faith, and the life lived out of that faith."[85] We do not merely hear parables; we participate in them.

But what is a parabolic theology? What does it mean to be midway between parable and systematic theology? Sallie McFague's description reflects many of the same characteristics and issues that we found in our discussion of the transnomic in therapy and social process. To begin with, it is a theology more concerned with metaphors and images than with concepts. It works with a different logic. A parabolic theology

> ought, for instance, to make theological discussions of the person of Jesus and the resurrection less "anxious" about logical precision, clarity, definiteness. This is not a call for fuzzy or sentimental thinking (or for saying nothing about difficult matters); on the contrary, to take metaphorical thinking seriously is a demand for precision and clarity, though not of the logical sort.[86]

Metaphor is the poet's way to try to define something for which the dictionary has no meaning, for which ordinary language is inadequate. Parabolic theology asserts that while discursive, linear, right-

83 Ibid., p. 41 (her emphasis).   85 Ibid., p. 3.
84 Ibid., p. 122.   86 Ibid., p. 39.

Towards a Transnomic Theology / 159

hemisphere thinking is the most recent in mankind's intellectual evolution, it is not necessarily the highest and most determinative form of human thought. It rejects the tyranny of systematic language in theological reflection, with the latter's lack of the basic forms of human thought in poetry, story, and symbol. Parabolic theology takes seriously the need to cultivate imagination. In short, it is a theology that speaks to the whole mind.

A parabolic theology is also one that will stress experience over concepts: "what is at stake in Christianity is not belief in doctrines correctly stated, but 'believing,' a process more like a story than it is like a doctrine."[87] Such a theology concentrates more on the process of coming to belief than on the beliefs themselves. She quotes with approval Richard R. Niebuhr: "believing is not commanded by beliefs. Beliefs come from believing; and believing is generated in experience."[88] Parabolic theology takes seriously the experience of theologians, for, while their lives are but moments in the ordinary world, they can still express something of ultimate truth. Consequently, autobiographical and confessional writings find a significant place in this style of theology.

Parabolic theology takes seriously its metaphorical, symbolic imaging, in our terms, its evoking character. It will, for instance, entail "a deformation of traditional symbols of Christianity, a placing of the symbols in a new context, so that they may again become metaphors, become revelatory."[89] Not surprisingly, McFague speaks appreciatvely of the rock opera *Jesus Christ, Superstar*. A parabolic theology is transnomic in calling us from the nomos to a deeper experience which eventuates in a new nomos from which, again, we shall need to be called. The whole process is one of adventure and risk, a call to the security found only in true faith. It acknowledges that there is no security in theology.

I believe that McFague has shared with us a spirit, an understanding, a vision by which to test our theologies in a quest for one which truly expresses what the Church *should* say about God, one which invites a constant reformation of its own structures even as it calls for an adventure beyond itself. She herself has not written such a theology nor have I. I, in this present effort, have merely pursued a series of pathways that seem ultimately to converge in an image of transnomic liberty. At best, this work probably remains at the stage

87 Ibid., p. 84.
88 Ibid., p. 142.
89 Ibid., p. 93.

found in Cobb and Driver, as an expression of the transnomic in service of the nomic. Perhaps theology will always be a nomic disciple, struggling to heed more fully the call to the transnomic.

I would not imply that religion has been unaware of the power of narrative. Most traditions have a long history of storytelling as a medium of instruction and nurture. This has been one important source of insight for therapy. Meditation practices bear strong similarities to some fantasy techniques. The stilling of the self, preparatory for mental imaging or free floating thought, is reminiscent of some Eastern disciplines and to the "centring down" of the Quakers. The Spiritual Exercises of St. Ignatius include mental imaging as a significant vehicle in faith development. Enacted story in the form of ritual has been a major instrument in the transmission of faith and the religious ordering of societies. Moreover, we should not conclude that the total theological task can be reduced to the telling of better stories and the evoking of more intense experiences. Theologians have a message to convey, a nomos to share, a faith to which they bear witness. They know that all stories do not necessarily heal, and that among those which do, some elicit a fuller humanness than others. If they are to be responsible to their convictions, they must seek some degree of critical self-awareness. They must ask what the story really means, even though the meaning will always transcend their interpretation. As Robert Hobson urges, we need to cultivate both the positivist and the romantic. "(Despite the vastly different methods of investigation) in human thought there is always a combination of fantasy thinking and directed thinking by means of imaginative insight."[90] In the vocabulary of transactional analysis, we need both experiencing in the Child and understanding in the Adult. Theologians have been compared to literary critics whose task is to develop a greater appreciation for the rich meaning in the faith story. Yet the very power of story in individual and social life should remind us of the primacy of narrative over its deciphered meaning, of the storyteller over the critic. Theology must keep alive its sense of narrative lest we end in an ongoing debate between critics about criticism and lose touch with the drama that gives life.

90 Hobson, "Imagination and Amplification in Psychotherapy," p. 100.

Index

Adler, Alfred, 42-43, 114
anomy, 74, 90, 92, 96-99, 104, 118-19, 134, 144, 153
anti-structure, 11, 72, 78, 82-83, 85, 88, 90, 92, 94-101, 104, 109, 117, 120, 135-36

Bandler, Richard, 50-51, 113
Barth, Karl, 139, 141, 143
Beardslee, William, 30
Berger, Peter, 72-73, 89-90, 92, 96, 104, 112-13, 115, 118, 137
Berne, Eric, 43
Bernstein, Joanne, 47
Bettleheim, Bruno, 46-47, 53-54, 104
Bonhoeffer, Dietrich, 146
Breuer, Josef, 41, 62
Brown, Judith, 47
Brown, Robert M., 120
Brunner, Emil, 106, 119
Buber, Martin, 98
Buechner, Frederick, 2, 94

Calvin, John, 108, 110, 119
Camus, Albert, 33

child/childhood, 15, 36, 41-44, 46, 48-49, 53-56, 59, 63-64, 74, 91, 94, 101, 118, 123, 153, 160
Cobb, John B., Jr., 9, 12, 31, 122, 127, 130, 138-51, 160
communitas, 11, 81, 88, 90-92, 94-102, 104, 111, 118, 120, 126, 133-36
counter-structure, 72, 78, 81, 85-86, 94-95
Crites, Stephen, 45, 68
Crossan, John D., 2, 10-11, 13, 15-38, 72, 78, 99, 104, 120, 140, 154, 157-58

Daly, Mary, 114
disruption, 10-11, 16, 18-22, 28, 30, 32-33, 35, 38, 53, 69, 72, 75, 78, 81, 101-104, 115, 117, 123, 154, 156
Driver, Tom, 9, 12, 122, 125, 127-43, 150-51, 160

Eliade, Mircea, 2
Erikson, Erik, 44, 104, 115

fantasy, 10, 13, 15, 36, 38-39, 41, 46, 54-69, 91, 102, 117-18, 154-55, 160
Fellner, Carl, 48-49, 53-54
Freud, Sigmund, 39, 41-43, 46, 54-56, 58, 61-62, 105, 114, 143, 156
Fromm, Erich, 56

Gardner, Richard, 48-49, 51, 54
Gordon, David, 50-52, 54, 66
Goulding, Mary and Robert, 44, 63-64, 117-18
Grimes, Ronald, 11, 75-77, 85-89, 156
Grinder, John, 50-51, 113

Haley, Jay, 52
Harré, R., 71
Hesse, Mary, 26-27, 29
Hillman, James, 40, 45, 47, 55, 66, 117
Hobson, James, 44, 66, 160
Hoffman, John C., 7, 40, 106n., 122-23

identity, 40-46, 54-55, 67-68, 72, 96, 104, 110, 114-15, 118-19, 136-37, 144, 155

Jaffe, Dennis, 58n., 62-68, 157
Jellinek, Augusta, 62n., 66, 117
Jung, Carl, 56, 61, 66

Kaufman, Gordon, 122
Keen, Sam, 2, 119
Kenner, Hugh, 34
Kort, Wesley, 2, 5
Kosbab, Paul, 61

law, 7-9, 12, 23-24, 103-21, 132, 137, 145
Leuner, H., 60-61
liminality, 10-11, 72, 78-102, 113, 115-16, 119, 133-34, 136, 154-55

Luther, Martin, 7, 105-106, 108-10, 112, 119, 129, 135
Lynch, William, 2

McClendon, James, 2
McFague, Sallie, 2, 153-55, 157-59
Machovec, Milan, 149
Malraux, André, 147-48
Marcel, Gabriel, 25
Mendenhall, George, 111-12
Merton, Robert, 73
Moltmann, Jurgen, 122-23
Mook, Bertha, 55
moralistic, 7-8, 103, 105, 123
myth, 2-3, 5, 16, 18, 29, 31-38, 42-43, 69, 100, 104, 112, 132, 158
mythic, 10-11, 31-38, 52, 69, 72, 78, 87, 99, 120, 132, 140, 146, 151, 154, 158
mythoparabolic, 10, 13, 37, 69, 72, 99, 104, 141, 154

Niebuhr, H. Richard, 138
Niebuhr, Reinhold, 98
Niebuhr, Richard R., 159
Nietzsche, F., 28
nomic/nomis, 12, 31, 73-74, 76-77, 85, 88-92, 96, 102, 110, 112-14, 125-26, 130-37, 139-40, 142-45, 150-57, 159-60
nomic bondage, 112-16, 119, 121, 124, 127-31, 139, 141, 143, 145, 151, 153
Novak, Michael, 2

Ornstein, Robert, 48, 58, 59n., 66

Panagiotou, Nancy, 63n., 66
Pannenberg, W., 121
parabolic, 10-11, 23, 25, 29-31, 33-37, 52, 72, 78, 97, 99, 105, 113, 117, 119-20, 123, 126-37, 140-41, 145-46, 149, 151, 154, 158
parabolic theology, 157-59

Peacock, James, 71, 72n.
Perls, Frederick, 61, 65
pilgrimage, 4, 11, 87-89, 91, 93, 95, 99, 101, 113, 133, 157
play, 10-12, 27, 30, 34, 36-37, 53-55, 61, 67-69, 91-93, 101, 104, 116, 118, 126, 154-55, 157
Popper, Karl, 26-29
Progoff, Ira, 44-45, 57, 58n., 60-62, 64, 66, 156

ritual, 2, 4, 11, 72-83, 88, 90, 98-102, 113, 133, 135, 155, 160
Rogers, Carl, 107
Rubenstein, Richard, 143

Sanders, E. P., 110-11
Satir, Virginia, 50-51
Secord, P. F., 71
Sheikh, Anees, 63n., 66
Siirala, Aarne, 39, 152, 157
Simonton, Carl and Stephanie, 44, 62-64
Slater, Peter, 2, 39, 125
Smart, Ninian, 2, 3
Soelle, Dorothee, 127
Soleri, Paolo, 150
structure, 10-11, 26, 28, 31, 49-50, 71-102, 104, 109-20, 127, 130, 133-37, 143-45, 150-51, 154-56
symbol, 4, 48, 56-58, 60-61, 69, 74-75, 85-87, 91, 159

Temple, William, 126
Tillich, Paul, 12, 30, 37, 96, 106-108, 116, 120, 124, 135-36, 154
transcendence, 10, 12, 25, 27, 29, 120
transmoral, 12, 96, 105-109, 115-16, 121, 123-24
transnomic, 10-12, 31, 90, 96, 109, 112, 115-27, 130, 132-37, 140-41, 144-46, 148, 150-60
Turner, Edith, 87, 88n., 90n., 91n., 93n., 95n., 97n.
Turner, Victor, 10-11, 71-102, 104, 111, 113, 115, 120, 133, 136, 154-56

unconscious, 40, 42, 46-49, 55-58, 61, 67, 101, 123, 155

van Gennep, Arnold, 78-79, 81
Via, Dan Otto, Jr., 16-20, 34, 36
von Rad, Gerhard, 153

Wainwright, Geoffrey, 153
Weber, Max, 94
Whitaker, Carl, 52, 54
Whitehead, A. N., 148, 151
Wiggins, James, 2
Wilder, Amos, 16, 32, 34, 36
Winnicott, D. W., 67-68, 104, 116, 118, 157